The Righting of Passage

CONTEMPORARY ETHNOGRAPHY

Kirin Narayan and Paul Stoller, Series Editors

A complete list of books in the series is available from the publisher.

The Righting of Passage

Perceptions of Change After Modernity

A. DAVID NAPIER

PENN

University of Pennsylvania Press

Philadelphia

53919602

10   9   8   7   6   5   4   3   2   1

Published by
University of Pennsylvania Press
Philadelphia, Pennsylvania 19104-4011

Library of Congress Cataloging-in-Publication Data
Napier, A. David.
    The righting of passage : perceptions of change after modernity/A. David Napier.
        p. cm. — (Contemporary ethnography)
    Includes bibliographical references (p.   ) and index.
    ISBN 0-8122-3776-5 (cloth : alk. paper)
    1. Ethnology—Philosophy. 2. Rites and ceremonies. 3. Social change. I. Title. II. Series.
    GN345.N365 2004
    306—dc22   2003068889

For Francis Huxley

Contents

Contents

Preface

"Men and women, entirely naked, circle around the king dancing lascivious dances. They strive to touch certain parts of his body with certain parts of theirs. It is not always possible to avoid contacts or to keep from contamination."

—*Paul Gauguin,* Noa Noa

Today, much thinking in the social sciences builds on the assumption that contemporary life, as the outgrowth of modernity, is characterized by high-speed, unexpected change—by unlikely juxtapositions and even by chaos. In such a world, we often hear, the ephemeral and translucent qualities of daily living create enough uncertainty that identity itself becomes discontinuous. Those who survive do so by limiting stress, by social networking, and by cultivating flexible identities that adapt readily to unexpected changes of circumstance. This is where, to recall Appadurai, the "soft" cultural forms (forms that "permit relatively easy separation of embodied performance from meaning and value") replace previously "hard" ones (where firm links exists "between value, meaning, and embodied practice"). Though it is not difficult for any of us to feel that this apparent change is, as it were, real, accepting life as an inevitably amorphous experience begs a fundamental question: if the contemporary world is as antistructural as postmodernists maintain, how can any of us structure our thinking enough to recognize or describe our experience of it?

If, in other words, one is enough of a postmodernist to believe that the world we inhabit is soft and antistructural, one must either accept the inability of any of us to structure our own sensations or, alternately, argue for some form of humanism that sees an inherently structured self living at odds with its unstructured environment. Indeed, the basic precondition of human communication—a parroting of the motor neurons of one ego by another (Adelberg n.d.)—is lost when chaotic social settings produce only chaotic flexible selves that have been denied, and therefore have never experienced, a self that is coherent. Were this emptiness universally actual, there would, a fortiori, be no coherent literature called "postmodern," and there would be no recognizable postmodernists to dissect such experience for us: no authors with coherent identities; no theories that could be communicated; no books bought or read;

no university departments dedicated to the industry of chaos. Without inter-action there is no risk (Schieffelin 1996; Howe 2000); without risk, no trans-formation (Napier 1986, 1992, 2003). In short, no ordered space for interpersonal understanding. This is the extreme premise that informs *The Righting of Passage*.

Instead of arguing, then, for the deep impact of flexible transnationalism on contemporary living, this book offers an ethographically based account of how modernity limits growth, as well as an intimation of how a coherent, commu-nicating self survives amid such apparent discontinuity. This it does by argu-ing something entirely counterintuitive to both modernist and postmodernist worldviews yet, somehow, still witnessed everywhere—namely, that the effect of separating embodiment from meaning in the postmodern world is actually the *slowing down* of human transformation. Here, the combined forces of stress management, depth psychology, therapeutic writing, institutional conformity, and apparent speed work together to produce a reduction—not a prolifera-tion—of change in human life.

The evidence for this reduction is everywhere, and its presence does, indeed, demonstrate the fact that something new is happening after modernity, but it may not at all be what we believe or had expected. Why, for instance, do those immensely popular and ubiquitous self-help programs we are all subjected to each begin with the invitation that we employ whatever technique is marketed to discover a place, a psychological centering, from which confidently to ground our actions? Why do pain clinics ask sufferers to find a mental image of some setting wherein each one of them can be comforted? Why are yogic practices advertised as meditative techniques for locating and grounding the self in a chaotic world? Why do therapists dealing with phobias and panic at-tacks employ hypnosis to create imaginary settings for the cultivation of men-tal security? The answer to each and all of these questions is, of course, that we are acutely aware of the need, as a shaman's apprentice might traditionally have been, to locate and cultivate a place of secure emotional attachment. At the same time, however, we also sense that our modern world moves so quickly that we continue to feel personally "groundless."

Moving all of the time most certainly undermines our ability to generate the attachments that hedge our bets against those failures which transformation and change, by definition, risk. While every Hindu on Bali has a temple of ori-gin (literally a "temple of the navel") with a symbolic umbilicus that can stretch only so far before snapping, we shop from therapy to therapy looking for a means to construct such a temple without knowing even where to put down the first stone. We intuitively understand, in other words, that the first step in con-fronting risk is best taken from a place where we are better balanced, but also that such places cannot be easily identified when we are moving all of the time in search of a better life. So, that absence of connectedness which seems so central to modern life makes changing all the more difficult and unlikely. This

is a powerfully shared feeling—perhaps powerful enough that the fearful resistance to change that is the outcome of such instability may be the only thing
that is truly new about postmodernity.

In the following pages, then, I sketch out the relevance of each of the above-
highlighted domains to what I see as a growing psychological entropy—a significant decrease, that is, in human psychological growth. In turn, I also argue
that the combined effects of these forces are a quantitative and a qualitative
decrease in our understanding of change as an embodied psychophysical experience. By forwarding this argument, it is my intention, at least initially, not
only to reframe a debate that has, as so many of us sense, run out of steam,
but also to stimulate others to take up the argument in more comprehensive
ways than this brief introduction will permit. On a more positive note, it is also
my hope that a modest reformulation of popular perceptions about what is
feasible can energize forces of growth that are yet unknown.

This book is, therefore, not only about developmental stasis but also about
the conventions we subscribe to that rationalize stasis. It is not only about static
forms of behavior that are now commonplace but also about the ways in which
stress and uncertainty have been codified as pathological. My working assumption here is that transformation is risky, and risk is, by definition, dangerous. Because of this truism we humans will, as Nietzsche so passionately (and
sometimes madly) argued, do whatever we can to resist change. Sometimes, as
in avoiding disasters, this attempt not to change is good and healthy. One
would not, for instance, advocate destructive change merely to unsettle something static. However, we each also attribute our most meaningful transformations to "going for" something that turns out well.

Because risk itself is morally ambivalent—at least until one has accepted
and acted upon it—the tendency to avoid it is also embedded in many otherwise laudable social conventions, and especially in institutional settings where
the regulating of behavior (that is, what is measured—literally, what is normal)
takes precedence over any and every form of destabilization, even those that
may result in productive change.

Institutional complacency, therefore, consistently undermines change even
among the most adventuresome of us—and, yes, also among those intellectuals (perhaps especially among those intellectuals) whose professional successes
are measured by how adventuresome they can appear to their institutional
peers. This is why, in a book about transformation, I have singled out narrators for a particular form of criticism, for they have devoted themselves to describing the risks others take—risks that they themselves (because of their
institutional loyalties) rarely invite, or confront only when they are rewarded
with moral capital.

If, that is, you have identified yourself as one who gives voice to another who
may have no social or institutional clout, the dangers are significant that your
"embodiment" may actually take the form of an appropriation—where the

use of the powerful narratives of others serves as much the interests of those of us who thrive on institutional networking as the interests of those who experience physically what we networkers recall through narrative. It is not only, therefore, that such appropriating serves to make heroes of those who might be inclined to exploit professionally the disadvantaged they write about (we do, after all, publish, perish, or otherwise textually memorialize ourselves) but that our so doing could, to recall Nichols, even become pornographic when it "plays," under the aegis of expository realism, with the bodies of others. Indeed, the aid industry is rife with visions of heroic glamour and self-promotion, where the outcome of human assistance is as much the glorification of the expositor or advocate as it is the betterment of some anonymous beneficiary of human goodwill. Narrators, therefore, have special obligations regarding the freedoms they exercise when mediating between their voiceless subjects and their readers.

Are we today any more culpable of such exploitation than people in other times? Is the problem, in other words, new? Whether more or less culpable, the circumstances of how we may be inclined to manipulate the tragedies of others are certainly different from what they once were, or at least arguably it seems thus; for today the tendency to appropriate is, if anything, exacerbated by what, for want of a better name, we have labeled the "postmodern condition"—where the belief that people live through narrative rules out so many other forms of embodiment that can make deep meaning possible.

It is convenient, in other words, to argue that literary texts have lives of their own (and that we can actually become the narratives we live by) only if we remain unwilling to accept that there may be life forms that are not fully knowable through reading or writing. While anthropology can provide us with examples of other modes of embodied meaning, there is nothing to cause us to relinquish our own cultural prejudices when the outcome would be a diminishing of the narrator's own status. Who after all wants to commit personal energy to idioms of meaning that are not valued in one's own culture, especially when the epic possibilities of writing, and the public audiences that recognition creates, appear so irresistible?

This is why part of this book focuses on the assumed forms of narrative realism that underlie ethnography (especially narratives of suffering and salvation) and on how institutions encourage us to think in quite prescribed and often limiting ways about the transformations of others. The book is, therefore, also about globalization, about postmodernism, and about anthropology; for these are the areas where the temptation to appropriate comes with the territory: in the first case (globalization), because freedom of movement (of people, of capital, and of institutions) across cultures serves a particular kind of order; in the second (postmodernity), because assuming that one can know nothing about others encourages a deeply solipsistic account of meaning; and in the third (anthropology), because an entire discipline so involves the descriptions of sensations that have not been embodied by its professional writers that members of the field are highly susceptible to appropriating (if unwittingly) the experiences of others.

But people who are in the midst of some profound transformation rarely codify in words what they are experiencing because its meaning may not be describable if they are humbled by what they cannot know, or if they are, as it were, de-centered by the Copernican knowledge that they cannot own, be the focus of, or otherwise embody what they witness. Yet this does not stop those of us with warm clothes and enough to eat from trumpeting the sorrows and weaknesses of the powerless subjects of our discourse. Here, of course, is where we get the Nietzschean part: where institutional "thinkers" feel compelled to align themselves with notable "doers" whom they perceive to be carrying out good work. In part they align themselves because they view with longing something that appears to be good and right; but in part they also do so to relieve themselves of the embarrassments of their own comfort. In elevating our narrative preoccupations, we not only discount other forms of embodiment, then, but we limit in turn our own willingness to explore how embodied meaning may be rendered, say, through the sense of smell or the exchange of food or by making love. It is because I am troubled by many habits of modern intellectual life (ones in which I myself participate) that this book will no doubt alienate many readers. It may alienate many scholars of the domains it addresses; and, indeed, it may well alienate many of my own friends and colleagues who have devoted themselves tirelessly to addressing the problems upon which this slim volume focuses.

This book is not, in other words, a systematic analysis of the complex literature on globalization, postmodernity, or narrativity, but a distillation of contemporary issues that look rather different when viewed from the perspective of growth and change. Because I set aside so many of the rulers of the domains I discuss, some readers may, I suspect, even find my views sweeping; or they may be discomfited by what they perceive to be my taunting of the sacred cows of both "liberal" and "conservative" social convention. They may, indeed, feel that I am simply wrong about the things I address. Oddly, I can agree at least on one level with such criticisms; for those wedded to the ways of modernity are right to say that there is no justification today for inducing yet more anxiety about who we are and what we do—especially when doing is already hard enough and when the risk of being critical leads to the accusation that one's views are anarchic or overly idealized or that one is spoiling the professional good life we all silently agree not to challenge.

However, if the reader at all senses that our lives today better demonstrate what is meant by the word "Mannerist" than did that polite movement in the sixteenth-century art world to which that term normally refers, we at least can make a start. For this book is about change and its absence; and change is sometimes brutal when it awakens us rudely—especially when we have, as we have today, so over-inscribed our so-called "global" social world that much of what in other times might have been called "serious debate" is precluded by imitative forms of social behavior that cloud human encounters and allow us, as Goffman once defined it, to "pass" for whatever identity produces a modicum of short-term anesthetic stability.

It is in this sense that we have become better Mannerists than those sixteenth-century painters—even if, or precisely because, we have forgotten the deep social need for manners; for the apparent forgetting that social obligation and good-neighborliness often require hard work (without guaranteed success or fame) is surely today at odds with the inscribed forms of meaning that we now privilege. So, the perceived aggressiveness of what follows should be read for the Liliputian attempt it is to wake for the briefest moment what looks to me like a loudly snoring giant. Those who know my writing know that I have other, more polite voices in print, but none of them has the tone I have reserved for this project.

Because the book is presented more polemically than other things I have written, I wish to express my gratitude to professional colleagues who agreed to my request that I experiment with each argument initially by writing a journal article or book chapter for a collected volume. To cultivate such a working style has required the support of many people and organizations. I therefore would like to acknowledge the individuals who invited me to write about the subjects I here take up.

First, accordingly, I would like to thank Paul Stoller, whose own *Sensuous Scholarship* has been a great source of inspiration, and James Wilce for inviting me to be a panel respondent and, later, volume commentator for *Social and Cultural Lives of Immune Systems* (Routledge, 2003). The first friendship has generated a wonderful dialogue about ethnography and illness writing, while the second allowed me to synthesize a number of social science responses to psychoneuroimmunology and, in turn, to develop the argument about culture and stress that I reframe as Chapter 1. Chapter 2 originated in an invitation from Conerly Casey and Robert Edgerton to contribute to their *Companion to Psychological Anthropology* (Blackwell, 2004). Chapter 3 began many years ago as a contribution to Susan DiGiacomo's edited volume *The Wounded Ethnographer* (Routledge, forthcoming); while Richard Grinker invited me to publish drafts of Chapters 4 and 5 in his "Social Thought and Commentary" section of *Anthropological Quarterly*.

Though the technique of publishing articles and commentaries as a way of assessing reader responses is common among trade writers, it is less usual in academic research, and I am therefore especially indebted to those colleagues who generously offered me a "first chance" to make a case that proved central to this book. Since so much of academic synthesizing is initially formalized before an audience of students, I am grateful to Vinay Jawahar of *Epilogue: Mid-*

dlebury Journal of Opinion for the invitation to vet my own Epilogue to this volume before the local student audience that galvanized its original formulation.

As my parents, Anthony and Pauline Napier, have informally listened to these arguments over two decades, I wish especially to thank them for their stubborn commitment to doing the right thing despite all odds; it is a formula I cannot say I have lived up to but one that I deeply admire. In addition, I would like to thank Michael Adelberg, Margaret Donlon, Cynthia Hernandez, Devon Jersild, John McWilliams, Emiko Ohnuki-Tierney, Paul Sender, David Stoll, Jonathan Sugar, and Reginald Young for their thoughtful and measured assessments of this project and for challenging me either to practice what I preach or acknowledge my limitations. I would like to thank Elizabeth Napier for assistance during the proofreading, and my son, Andrew, and daughter, Harriet, for patiently waiting through the many months during which I stared at a computer screen. I would also like to thank Andrew Lemert for alerting me to the more pugilistic dimensions of the authorial voice I at times am taken by, and William Douglass, whose *Casting About in the Reel World* uses his skills as an angler to show how, in any contest, releasing one's prey is as important as catching it. If in this slim volume I have less artfully cast my opinions and released what vexes me most, I must all the more express my thanks to these individuals for their assistance, friendship, and support.

Finally, I would like to thank my long-time friend Francis Huxley for showing me how a mind can be both ruthlessly inquisitive and inherently kind. It is to him, therefore, that I have dedicated this book.

Chapter 1

Dressed to Kill

The individual who has not risked his life may well be recognized as a person, *but he has not attained the truth of this recognition.*

—*Hegel,* Phenomenology of Spirit

Stressful Encounters

Not long ago, on an expedition to a video store with my then-twelve-year-old son, I was taken aback by a frightening display of a new interactive game that invites one to engage in cellular warfare as an embodied microorganism. Players in this virtual battleground can project themselves into the very mitochondria that convert the energy provided by food into the energy that cells employ while engaging in their own versions of Armageddon.

My first reaction was the typical one of a wary parent in an altogether unhealthy place: what, I thought, could possibly be the benefit of my son's sitting in front of a television moving his thumb and forefinger for hours on end while the rest of the muscles in his body cried out for what we Americans call quality time? What is it like to play a video game in which one is able to assume the role of mitochondria or of protein envelopes? Will these experiences actually benefit our abilities to think creatively, or are they merely dulling experiences that make us duller still? All I could think about was the view I had so often heard expressed: that this kind of activity was, in total, wholly unhealthy.

For sure, I would have probably never challenged this argument had the virtual spaces I witnessed been inhabited by the usual array of graphic war games, sports competitions, and science fiction. But the presence of those mitochondria drew to my attention an immediate irony: namely that these very kinds of battle images—the ones to which we attribute so many of the social ills of today—were precisely of the sort that in psychoneuroimmunology (PNI) had been touted as health-inducing stimulants for cancer sufferers.

The idea of visualizing the defeat of pathogens has for some time now been promoted as a means of stimulating active immune responses. That antibody production can be stimulated through visual imagery has, in fact, been enough acknowledged that at least one entire professional journal (*Journal of Mental Imagery*) exists to publicize research on the relationship between mental imagery and human understanding. Let children, for instance, engage in video warfare in which they can, say, reduce white blood cell counts and promote in them a positive outlook on their potential for surviving cancer—or, at least, that is the working assumption.

So, what is ironic in this? Well, nothing really, if the victory one experiences produces a sense of success and well-being. Where the irony enters is in our common belief that stress, *in and of itself*, is unhealthy. How many heart attacks are attributed by families and friends to stress? How many meditation training courses are based upon the belief that relaxation promotes immunity? Putting aside our very notion of being "stressed out," how much research in psychoneuroimmunology (from Ader and Cohen onward) is predicated on the assumption that stress is debilitating and that it is, by definition, harmful to immunity?

Yet, if stress is harmful to immune function, why do athletes remain healthy? Why do CEOs miss the fewest days of work on account of sickness? Why do so-called "invincible kids" transcend sometimes horrid familial circumstances to become productive members of society? Why do people attribute their most meaningful transformations in life to events that are often stressful? The answer, of course, is simple. It is because these all are instances in which the experience of stress produces a positive, empowering outcome. These are cases, in other words, where the results of a stress-induced transformation are positive rather than negative, and they are, all of them, mitigated by the ontological setting within which they unfold. Rats that display addictive behavior in a particular controlled environment will, as Peele has beautifully demonstrated (1985), elect for transcending their pathologies when that controlled space includes colorful objects and additional stimuli. Color the walls of the "rat park," throw in a few rusty cans to play with, and mix the genders of the caged animals—that is, diversify the otherwise controlled environment—and suddenly the rats' supposed drug "addiction" drops radically.

Context, in other words, not only defines stress, but also turns pathologies into creative encounters; for it is the *context* of the stressful event, not merely one's response to a given stressor, that determines whether stress will be a catalyst for a beneficial transformation or a harbinger of disaster. The former we see regularly in what are often called "religious experiences," the latter in so-called "illnesses." As structures of personal change, of course, the two are indistinguishable. Both, that is, are profound forms of transformation, profound moments when individuals are brought to the threshold of a cathartic transformational moment; but one turns out beautifully, the other more often than not abysmally. They seem opposite to us; yet as the anthropological literature on rites of passage amply demonstrates, in form they are so alike. Shamans throughout the world and over the aeons have repeatedly reminded us that our successes are not measured by avoiding stress, but by orchestrating it creatively. This is why shamans always receive their powers to heal through trials that are potentially disastrous (Narby and Huxley 2000).

As so many shamanic legends graphically visualize for us, the smaller the pieces into which the shaman is torn, the greater his or her transcendental power—if, that is, the shaman survives the encounter. Like the body of Parvati, whose parts are each assigned to a different Indian temple, the more extreme and wide-ranging the breakup, the more power attributed to the goddess and by extension, the pilgrim who embodies her through years of pilgrimage. At the same time, the risks have to be significant: for the greater that centrifugal explosion, the greater the possibility that all the king's horses and all the king's men will never, as it were, put Humpty together again.

The unpredictability of stress is then crucial for recognizing and acknowledging the veracity of change—for embodying the paradox of both being oneself and something new. The more one can predict an outcome, the less change that is likely to have taken place. This is why those concepts we regularly employ to explain change—like evolution, for instance—can never stand as theories of change, or indeed as theories at all, in the sense of possessing rules that have predictive value—why evolutionary "challenges," to extend this example, are recognized only in retrospect as either destructive or enhancing. In fact, the ambivalence of stress is so important that one might even claim that the goal of each of our lives is to orchestrate stressful events so that they have a productive rather than a destructive end.[1] This may indeed be why life's struggles will always possess a deeply moral dimension.

Realizing the *ambivalence* of stress and its transformations is then deeply important. First, it is important because the specificity of science—and especially its tendency to fetishize quantitative measures—frequently devalues those repetitive social stressors whose effects are variable, cumulative, and not easily measured. Second, the actual ambivalence of stress is important because all too often we look back upon events that have bad outcomes and only then label them as stressful. The ones that turn out good, on the other hand, get narratively reframed in ways that normalize them—that align them with paradigms of well-being that suppress their initial danger and uncertainty. That is why illness regularly is equated with chaos and disaster while stressors that produce satisfying outcomes get absorbed in adaptive narratives of growth and health, if not of spirituality and religion. Stress gets identified with cathartic changes that are largely negative while happiness homogenizes potential disorder into stories that are at odds with the often-unsettling nature of everyday life.

One of the major hurdles for stress research (as in the field of PNI) is to find ways in which the complex origins of illness outcomes—that is, the "algorithms" of stress—can be studied experimentally. In Bali, for instance, the *ben-*

efits of destabilizing and paroxysmal trance states are contrasted to the awareness that repeated exposure to decontextualized stressors—stressors that are
not catalysts for growth—either overstimulate a person, or wear one down.
Everything here depends on the social context in which stressful experiences are
carefully orchestrated. For the Balinese to study stress as a specific stimulus to
a measurable response would be to fail to understand its meaning entirely.

For science then so much of the problem of understanding stress relates directly to the artificiality of the experimental method, to the sterility of laboratory life, to experiment rather than to experience. Compare the Balinese view
of stress (for example, Howe 2000; Napier 1986, 1992; Wilce 2003; Wikan
1990) to the experimental method: now each time one introduces an additional variable into one's lab work, each time one lets the lab animal wander
around the neighborhood, one threatens to contaminate the controlled conditions of experimentation and, in so doing, to undermine the verifiable methods that are the basis of scientific truth. Indeed, one might even argue that the
specificity that is characteristic of the experimental method in itself limits our
ability to do justice to the social variables at work. An individual suffering the
stress of a leg fractured while saving a child from a speeding car has a much
different view of the outcome of his or her stress from the individual who
broke the exact same bone after plunging down a tenement staircase that a
slumlord failed to repair. In these two circumstances, in other words, the same
biological stressor—the broken leg—has two radically different outcomes. As
Lyon points out in her contribution to the aforementioned volume of Wilce,

There is little attempt in the PNI literature to deal with questions of social action or
agency, even though lip service is given to action through such terms as "behavior" and
"psychosocial factors." . . . What is offered by PNI is a concatenation of terms that do
not constitute a theoretical or experimental integration of domains—social, physical,
functional. Thus, in the framework given, social forms of explanation cannot be
brought to bear on biological mechanisms and vice versa. This is an obvious point, yet
it is frequently overlooked in discussion of the capacities of psychoneuroimmunology
to bridge psycho-social and bodily domains. (2003:84)

Sometimes, in fact, it is hard to resist the paranoid view that the field of PNI
research was itself started as a means of limiting the authority of social explanations precisely at the moment when they seem most applicable—to repossess
a domain that bench scientists felt to be slipping from their tightly controlled
experimenting!

So, the methods of scientific research themselves may in part at least be to
blame for the limited impact of social explanations on scientific discourse. To
create an experimental climate where, for example, an event's effects on hor-
monal activity can be measured is not in and of itself to have quantified stress.
Furthermore, as we will see later in this book, it is not only understanding the
limits of controlled experimentation that denies us access to what might, oth-

erwise and elsewhere, have been a truism of change; for the controlled environments of social institutions readily produce the precise same limitations.

These observations seem so obvious and self-evident that stepping back a bit from all of the media hype around stress and immunity, one is shocked by the absence of interdisciplinary research in which the social and psychological dimensions of psychoneuroimmunology are attended to with the same degree of thoroughness as the many volumes of tendentious research in which the questionable belief that "types" of people are cancer-prone not only goes unexamined, but is handsomely funded by our governments and universities.[2]

Here, the recent psychosomatic research on hypertension seems especially informative; for with hypertension we see how the traditional view of psychosomatic conditioning—that perceived emotional distress repeatedly raises blood pressure and causes sustained hypertension—cannot be confirmed at the empirical level of social fact. Indeed, as Mann has amply demonstrated, there appears to be at best a weak link between anger and/or anxiety and acute hypertension, and perhaps even an *inverse* relationship between perceived emotional distress and hypertension, despite popular belief and decades of research claiming that such a connection exists (1996, 1999a, 1999b).

Setting aside for a moment the profound impact that such research might have for, say, the therapeutic uses of biofeedback and meditation, the easy lesson in these findings suggests a much more plausible connection between the *isolation* or *dissociation* of emotional states and paroxysmal hypertension. Survivors of severe trauma, for instance, who uniformly insisted that such experiences "had no lingering impact on them" were more frequent sufferers of severe and symptomatic paroxysmal hypertension than those who simply "freaked out" over life's turmoils. Actually, these social factors are so central that it is now widely believed that emotional support is more relevant to surviving a heart attack than are any of the risk factors traditionally associated with myocardial infarction, including cholesterol levels, blood pressure, and even smoking. We have known for some time that anaesthetized patients undergoing surgical procedures have better outcomes when polite language is used in the operating theater and that, conversely, individuals experiencing shock will have poorer outcomes when family members mourn their suffering. Why not then step out of the lab for a moment to discover how the actual living of life does, indeed, influence the effects of stress on each of us?

That recognizing these relationships goes back to Cannon's days (1942) and more recently to Kleinman's call for an interpretive approach to healing that is socially integrated (1980) seems, however, not to have resulted in the serious attending to the influences that the social has upon the physical by those who are wedded to what Latour and Woolgar have labeled "laboratory life" (1979). At the same time, studies that begin with therapeutic premises that are culturally informed (for example, among many others, Csordas 1994, Danforth

1989, or Wikan 1990) so reshape the object of intellectual reflection that scientists commonly fail to acknowledge such research as clinically relevant.

Perhaps then it may yet become wholly obvious why we need to face the individual and social powers of placebos (Harrington 2000; Moerman 2002)—where the care and the giving mean as much as what is given. Perhaps we may even finally accept how, as Moerman so cogently puts it, "meaning is the inescapable complementary medical treatment" (2000:65).

The Ghost of Descartes

To say that meaning per se is what makes stress either life-enhancing or destructive may be merely to offer a truism that is as unsatisfying as it is obvious. However, the essential premise of PNI—indeed, of social psychology itself—is that the linkage between body and behavior is mitigated by social meaning, and that our understanding of this linkage must go well beyond any kind of simple measurement of how body and behavior correlate. This means, of course, not only that we become aware of how meaning is refined in local, social settings, but that we account for the various ways in which identity itself is socially, culturally, and individually negotiated.

The fact that none of these domains lend themselves to the sort of easy commonality that is basic to experimentation provides one obvious reason why so-called "social factors" emerge in stress research more in the form of lip service than in that of serious scientific discourse. At the same time, we at least can accept the fact that transformational processes cannot be understood without some real sense of how both individuals and collectives define the ontological domains in which these processes are shaped. Studying the nature of contemporary human change and of our perceptions about change require, therefore, not only an examination of the variation of transformational processes in different social settings and over time, but of concepts of personhood, and of how certain forms of personhood are acknowledged, stigmatized, or even prohibited by the social institutions we live by. These domains, therefore, provide a broad outline of the focus of this small volume; but they also beg the question of just how "social factors" do play out for each of us, especially when meaning is—as postmodernists would have it—reduced to fragmented and peculiarly individualized experiences.

At one extreme, the postmodern denial of the reality of shared ways of living leaves us with little more that existential despair to assuage our sense of personal isolation. But the fact that our modern world may be made up of autonomous Cartesian selves and others (ten Have 1987) in no way exhausts the possible constructs that may, and have been, applied to the experience of being human in other cultural settings. To claim, in other words, that one cannot speak of culture—because the range of social meaning is infinite—is merely to excuse us from having to engage in the sometimes fatiguing work of developing another complex and unfamiliar mode of understanding. It may even be the case that social explanations will never be brought fully to bear on biological mechanisms so long as the body is understood only as a wholly autonomous and socially independent agent. At the same time, the Cartesian nature of how we see ourselves need not prohibit us from recognizing that a broader view of emotion might provide multiple models of how the social and the biological are variably shaped by our responses to those catalytic moments we label as stressful. Our shared perceptions of what makes a person are, therefore, critical to how we interpret stress, because stress by nature elicits an anxiety about, if not an assessment of, one's ontological condition.

So, two people playing the same video game of cellular war may have totally different responses to their respective visceral projections. For one person, it might be a dulling, mechanically repetitive activity that is actually numbing while for another, or for that same person in another setting, the same stimulus might be the very vehicle for inducing a positive transformation. We have seen both arguments convincingly made—a fact that, in itself, ought to alert us to the possibility that something much deeper is going on when we examine stress. In the face of the laboratory conditions that gave rise to Ader and Cohen's landmark work, we must then place Peele's equally provocative finding that an addictive stimulus can have a radically different outcome if we modify the social setting in which that stimulus is experienced (1985:79 ff.). In West Africa, female circumcision may have deep cultural meaning while in America it is nothing more than genital mutilation. For the Sioux Native American, a vision quest makes enlightenment possible through imposed hardship; for that Native American's psychiatrist, the patient is merely a troubled masochist. What are these differences if not "social"?

Going through the motions without the right "spirit" then quickly changes the meaning of a creative activity into something less encouraging. The difficulty for illness experiences is that the odds of manipulating the experience of ill-health into a life-giving kind of change seem, and so often are, overwhelming. Though illness is by definition undesirable, it shares with love its transformative power. So, what is lost in seeing illness monolithically (as only a saddening moment in an otherwise happy life) is the reality of change—the fact that transcending hardship can be a hugely fulfilling experience in even the dullest moments of daily living. Why don't we then look at illness more positively? The answer is, first of all, because our images and metaphors for illness are also monolithically appalling: body warfare, loss of self-control, giving up one's body to the invader—that is, our dominant images are defeating us from the outset (Napier 2003). And second, because illness is, well, sickening: it is simply naive to promote in the face of genuine suffering a "don't-worry-be-happy" message, such as one may readily find in all of the self-help and recovery books that say "feel good and you'll get better."

Let's face it, serious illnesses are mostly not transcended. For every Lance

Armstrong who turns cancer into a catalyst for winning the Tour de France, there are thousands who succumb. And then there are the heroic epithets we apply to unanticipated transcendence. In our efforts to make him more than mortal, we cover up the fact that something happened *within the illness experience itself* that allowed him to love who he was—that made it possible for him to see the beauty in the video game he had crawled into. He *wanted* to discover some new dimension of experience and he was lucky enough to discover it or believed strongly enough to see the discovery of it when he found its door unlocked.

Why do we appear so culturally unaware of the ambivalent nature of stressful encounters? Why, at the molecular level, do we suppress the true sympathy between antigen and antibody that is necessary for their induced binding? In immunology, I suspect, this suppression occurs primarily because our culturally preferred ways of describing transformational encounters leave no room for ambivalence, real though its transformational role may be. We see warfare and hatred everywhere, even if the facts of molecular induction prove that metaphors of vaccinology—the assimilation of difference rather than its elimination—fit what can be observed much better that do the self/nonself models of immunology and virology.

In such cases, recognizing the limited accuracy of immunological models of cell-cell relations in no way helps us to understand why culturally we think of encounters with pathogens as *only* sickening. So, the moment a Lance Armstrong surfaces, all we know how to do is glorify him, even though his illness may be as conditioning as it is punishing; we suppress, in the end, the awareness that his pathogens actually had a highly *creative* impact upon his wellbeing. Our views of stressful events, in other words, change just as much as we ourselves are changed by them—so much so, in fact, that *time* itself becomes an essential ingredient in the codification of a stressful event's meaning. Besides, it is just so much easier for us to construct an idea of Lance Armstrong as a genetically superior being than it is to acknowledge the many athletes who do not succeed in transcending their illnesses.

Indeed, when we begin to look at a particular form of stress as a catalyst (positive or negative) for social transformation, we also begin to recognize that the meaning of a stressful event not only changes over time, but changes quite variably from one individual to the next. Later in this volume (Chaps. 4 and 5), we will examine cases that clearly show not only how variable today are the durations of the transformations that stress galvanizes, but we will also see how the power of change is itself a direct function of the *unpredictability* of any given transformation.

Stress may, as we say, put people "over the top," but it can also be the very event that moves any one of us *over time* to become committed—even against all odds—to making the apparent flaw of suffering into the centerpiece of the art of living. What we are witnessing, in other words, is a transformation, a rite of passage, but one that in a contemporary setting may take enough years to unfold that its transformational nature escapes us entirely.

The outcome of stress, then, has as much to do with our sense of what its experience might give way to—our feelings about it over quite variable lengths of time—as it does with the immediate influence it may have upon us in a controlled setting. What else, besides the way we contextualize a specific stressor, can account for how we ascribe to that experience a particular meaning? And what better a context than those symbolically heightened moments that—before the behavioral sciences destroyed the word—we used to affiliate with "ritual"?

Dressed to Kill

"Confronting cancer," writes Stoller of his own illness experience, "is a frighteningly lonely proposition" (forthcoming). "How do you confront your isolation? How do you face your fate? Songhay sorcerers have one suggestion; they say that you should diligently perform personal rituals. . . . [for] when we are able to perform these personal rituals, they give us a good feeling. They make us feel, if only for a little while, that we can generate and maintain a measure of control over our lives." Why ritual? After all, considerable effort in contemporary anthropology has been devoted to denouncing the sensational displays associated with ritual events in favor of elevating the mundane worlds of everyday living. But choosing the secular in favor of the sacred misses completely Stoller's—and his Songhay sorcerers—point: given the choice between potentially more or potentially less meaning, only the insensitive would choose, when stress comes calling, to jettison a deeper symbolic world for an everyday one. In this view, the everyday becomes meaningful by ritualizing it—by, if you will, generating an obsessive compulsion about the need to import symbolic depth and embodied sensuousness into an otherwise vacuous social space. To make meaning in the confines of a dreary and dehumanizing clinical setting, in other words, one must work hard to "ritualize" socially powerful metaphors—metaphors, indeed, that only have meaning because their socially shared nature has been repeatedly demonstrated. Ritual then, as Houseman and Severi also show (1998), is not an "unreal" mode of living, but a very special kind of social activity that most modern secularists are at a loss to understand.

In a world where experience on its own will not suffice—where experience must be "lived" to have meaning; in a world where the living of life is not enough—where life must be "real" to be true, and those "real life" "lived experiences" are held up as transcendent—simply saying that something has more meaning, or is more "real," is considered an adequate testament to its veracity. "I am telling you such-and-such *and I really mean it*." If, in other words, we fail to understand the ways in which the rituals of a culture at large get imported into private ceremony, the chances are slim that we will ever understand how a compulsive act may also be a creative one.

Though the long-term outcomes of stress must then be viewed outside of the limited world of laboratory life, both the physical embodiment of culture and the diversity of individual forms of its embodiment have been recognized for decades. Setting aside the capacity of social circumstances anywhere and at any time to influence perceptions of well-being, we see already in Cannon's landmark *Wisdom of the Body* (1932) how even the advent of household heating can undermine the role of shivering in inducing body temperature adjustment and, hence, human adaptation (Napier 2003). And, today, allergic rhinitis, that chronic inflammation of nasal passages affecting 40 percent of children and 20 to 30 percent of adults, is now widely attributed to the desensitizing influence of early immunization and the common hygienic practices that result in an over-reaction to local allergens (Guzman 2001). Now even the actual place of food production and the transport of potential allergens in and out of local ecologies have been blamed for sensitizing populations that could be desensitized by the simple act of eating locally produced foods and by consuming the locally produced honey in which allogenic local proteins are carried (Cone and Martin 1998)!

Thus, though it is obvious that scientists largely pay only lip service to "social factors" in the neuroimmunology of diseases, it is clearly the case that social conditions do have profound effects on an organism's ability to adjust to its environment. These examples—and there are countless others—illustrate dramatically how our social practices and related beliefs about how we live together and interact do have a significant influence on the body's ability to respond to environmental stressors, and, consequently, on the conditions of suffering and illness. This being the case, the obverse is also true: namely, that our beliefs about what makes a person will contribute over time to social forms that enhance or limit the proliferation of certain pathologies.

Are there then, as it were, "Cartesian" diseases? Most definitely; for if we live in a world in which the sense of smell is blunted in 40 percent of our children because our antiseptic lives have blunted their bodies' abilities to be environmentally conditioned, then the beliefs about personhood that alienated us from those stimuli must be the cause of the very proliferation of those same diseases. Placed now against an "immunological" masterplot in which a "self" survives by recognizing and eliminating "nonself" (Napier 2003), one can begin to picture the scope of this metaphysical disaster.

The "Yes, but . . ." reaction of our folks in white lab coats cannot, in fact, alter this simple reality, and one must wonder about the extent to which the fears of nuclear holocaust—all of the "ducking" and "covering" to which our baby-boom kids were subjected—has had its toll on the alarming rise in autoimmune disorders. What better an illness form than "the stranger within" to accommodate the paranoid demonology of not only being taken over by an external agent, but of actually mistaking self for nonself? As Lasch points out

(1984:44), "the dominant imagery associated with political protest in the sixties, seventies, and eighties is not the imagery of 'personhood,' not even the therapeutic imagery of self-actualization, but the imagery of victimization and paranoia, of being manipulated, invaded, colonized, and inhabited by alien forces." Here, I would like to call attention to a well-known example described at length in Johnson's *The Body in the Mind* (1987:6) in which the author argues that nearly all traditional semantic theory is dominated by a kind of objectivism in which imagination is thought to be completely irrelevant to the specification of meaning. Because of this literal focus, we tend, Johnson argues, to ignore, or at best to undervalue, the sort of semantic phenomena that are central to metaphors, or to any other sorts of "nonpropositional and figurative structures of embodied imagination" (xxxv). A number of philosophers and social scientists concerned with the nature and function of metaphor have, likewise, argued that metaphoric thinking is not always reducible either to rational propositions or to literal concepts (for example, Kirmayer 1992), and that what is ignored by such reductive thinking is precisely the ways in which embodied structures of imaginative thought actually influence human behavior. As Johnson puts it, "imagination seems to exist in a no-man's-land between the clearly demarcated territories of reason and sensation" (xxix).[3]

Part of the problem with neglecting the cultural embodiment of imaginative constructs is that such neglect makes it possible for potentially unhelpful metaphors to take root socially and to overwhelm us. The second major problem is that our outright rejection of the personal significance of these metaphoric categories, and our consequent alienation from their negotiated meaning, encourages us to see their role in stressful settings as only harmful. Third, our view of stress as mostly harmful discourages us from encounters with others whom we find alien or just different.

But without getting close to those outsiders one cannot measure them. So, will what I have elsewhere called "The Age of Immunology" necessarily have the effect of creating future illnesses that are yet more "Cartesian"—where our inability to see the "selfness" of the "other" is limited by our postmodern tendency to focus yet more on our isolation? Almost certainly, unless we find other ways of transforming our tendency to work as hard as possible to undermine our very humanity. While Lasch himself could wax nostalgic about that once-autonomous individual whose responsible behavior was the outcome of the exercise of free will, even he recognized the need to acknowledge the contingent nature of identity; for "if people programmed as white Anglo-Saxon protestants cannot enter vicariously into the lives of people programmed as blacks or Indians or Chicanos, experience loses the quality of contingency not only in the sense that cultural 'conditioning' rules out freely initiated actions but in the sense that one person's experience no longer connects in any way with another's" (161). Here our thinking of the body as a battleground in which "otherness" is routinely eliminated by cells that are, as it were, "dressed to kill" has the effect of causing us to think of stress as only a debilitating thing. Here, too, the alienation from shared meaning that so many postmodernists lay claim to as a testament to their own sensitivity begins to look more like yet one more example of giving in to a pathetic intolerance for ambiguity. Saying, in other words, that nothing can be collectively shared is shown, after the lights are turned up, to be nothing more than having excused oneself from ever having to negotiate with those who are, indeed, genuinely beyond that little bubble we are each meant to inhabit.

In fact, the evidence that we may have so given in to our exclusion of dif-ference is probably most powerfully witnessed when we repeatedly make one alien into another kind of alien even when we try to normalize or assimilate those we take to be different or to have different, or special, needs. An excel-lent example of this tendency is found in what was, in the mid-1970s, a legiti-mate desire to include handicapped school children in the mainstream of public school education (Stone 1993:53).

Under the Education for All Handicapped Children Act of 1975, public school systems are required to identify children with disabilities, to make special accommodations for them, and to educate them in the "least restrictive environment," meaning that they are to be integrated in regular classrooms whenever possible. Because the statute also pro-vided for federal funds to local schools on a per-handicapped child basis, it created enormous incentives for the development of personnel and methods to identify handi-capped children. The law had the ironic (but entirely predictable) effect of leading to the identification of *more* children as handicapped and of having more children edu-cated for at least part of the day in separate classrooms apart from the "mainstream."[4]

Like the current abuses of sedatives for "attention deficit" and "hyperactive" schoolchildren, the tendency to feel collectively as if we are all outsiders be-comes irresistible; for without the ability to negotiate the subtle domain where self and other merge, we find ourselves incapable of living with ambiguity. In-deed, the tendency to alienate all of us is so powerful that in the aforemen-tioned example the outcome was startling, if not surprising. Within the ten years following the act, the learning-disabled population rose by an alarming 142 percent, "so that at the end of the period learning-disabled students made up 44 percent of the total" (54).[5] If nothing else, this example goes to show that you cannot legislate equality when paranoid and alienating clinical metaphors dominate social interactions. If we are all "outsiders," there is no need to look beyond the self because one cannot, by definition, do so. Herein sits squarely the paradox by which we homogenize the exotic by denying its incommensu-rability and, simultaneously, seek to exclude and ultimately eliminate from our paranoid world anyone who strikes us as different. In this sense, the postmod-ern program can be, as we will see, as much a reactionary and predictable in-tellectual initiative as it is a theoretically innovative one—another apology, as it were, for an unwillingness to risk encountering the unknown, a fearful para-noia about one's own alienation.

Can we make too much of this paradox by which we both homogenize and alienate difference? Hardly; for without addressing its impact on how we approach that catalyst called "stress," we have no way of assessing the depth of its consequences for our concepts of personhood and our understanding of how those concepts have concrete outcomes for the longevity of our species. Can we make too much of the depth and pervasiveness of contemporary social paranoia? Perhaps the old-fashioned cultural categories that social anthropologists once enthusiastically studied are not as tidy as one might have liked, but stress always does have a way of crystallizing what is and is not socially shared. After an initial surge of interest among young adults in careers as firemen and policemen following the New York and Washington bombings of September 11, only the CIA noted a sustained rise in recruits.

Chapter 2

Self and Other in an "Amodern" World

Hegel tells us that the self is born only in battle with another consciousness, through a struggle with the Other.

—*Massey,* Birth of the Self, *126*

The Category of the Person

It is often said that social anthropology is the study of no more nor less than the modes of thinking by which a cosmology gives way among individuals to forms of embodied practice. In such a view, the act of examining another way of life must be based upon some willingness to consider the possible experiential differences that a galaxy of shared perceptions makes feasible. Out of such a structural sensibility, the notion of "culture" arose during the Enlightenment as the study of life-forms and, in our era, of the lives of those individuals whose minds were inhabited by idiosyncratic manifestations of what were understood as shared cultural perceptions.

But already in the early twentieth century, it had been forcefully argued that the possible variations of any particular life-form might be infinite—or at least that they could appear to be so—and given this variability, that the proper domain of sociology ought rightly to *exclude* those psychological factors that accounted for perceptual variations among individuals. Durkheim was clear on this point,[1] as were so many others who believed that the focus of our field of inquiry could be located in recognizing and elucidating the categorical mechanisms that framed the various images of the world that we each individually drew.

Much of the growth of British social anthropology—and of its younger cousin, American cultural anthropology—could be outlined as an outcome of this fundamental discrimination. However, the very French social theory that defined these parameters soon produced its own debunking; for the clear counterargument was made that the distinction between individuals and shared perceptions was itself a cultural construct. This construct, it turned out, could be easily challenged by the indisputable awareness that any one of us could only know the manner in which we individually embodied anything (because the only thing of which we have both subjective and objective knowledge was the very body we each inhabit)[2] and because the growing corpus of ethnographic literature provided numerous examples of cultures in which the notion of the person was itself ameliorated by various claims on that notion's autonomy.[3]

In fact, it was the latter of these two that was first recognized in the repeated instances in which Cartesian ideals were struck down by the daily living of life elsewhere[4]—first this recognition, of course, because it is always easier to recognize difference in another than in oneself.[5] Perhaps the most gifted of all expositors of these now "cultural" differences was the French cleric and ethnographer Maurice Leenhardt, who, by virtue of his experience in Melanesia over some four decades, was able to offer stunning examples of other modes of thinking that could challenge Descartes at every turn—examples unusual enough that they may never be equaled in the anthropological literature. Indeed, Leenhardt's expository skills were born out of a fascination and love that could only result from being himself so thoroughly transformed by the anthropological enterprise.

Here is one famous example (Leenhardt 1937:195):

Un jour que, sous ces impressions, je voulais mesurer cependant le progrès accompli chez ceux que j'avais instruits de longues années, je dis à l'un d'eux:
    —En somme, c'est la notion d'esprit que nous avons porté dans votre pensée.
    —Pas du tout, objecta-t-il brusquement, nous avons toujours connu l'esprit. Ce que vous nous avez apporté, c'est le corps.
    —????[6]

Leenhardt time and again offered compelling cases in which a body image, and its boundaries, were enough negotiable so as nearly to *require* outright condemnation on the part of any psychoanalyst who might find himself trapped into fitting an alien worldview into his experiences at the couch. In "La Personne mélanésienne," Leenhardt makes his view unequivocally: "Un personnage est une figure et un rôle. . . . Il ne discrimine pas entre le corps et le rôle" (1942 [1970], 104).[7]

So compelling were such cases from the daily experiences of ethnographers that few if any psychological theorists dared allow themselves to be ensnared into "explaining away" what to all others seemed mysterious and at times ineffable. Indeed, in Hindu Bali, the body-image boundary seemed fluid enough that a state of possession could be linked not only to the active overtaking of the self by another with whom that self had interacted, but that the distance between positive and negative magic could dissolve in a phenomenal encounter the moral value of which could not be known as it was experienced. Here, time and again, a vanquished spirit would even thank its vanquisher for being released from a life cycle that caused even its best intended actions to have destructive outcomes.

No less than Gregory Bateson, perhaps the most innovative of all ethnographers of the last century, realized that abandoning his psychological inquiries on Bali was necessitated both by the way in which the complexities of Balinese thinking defied the potential range of his own intellectual gymnastics and by the problem of how one might translate what his experiences suggested into a language that fellow westerners could appreciate. But his then-wife Margaret Mead did attempt this translation; and, though she no doubt started the contemporary women's movement by so doing for middle America, eventually she suffered the approbation both of her professional peers, who considered her work unverifiable, and, eventually, of a women's movement, which found her interest in gender differences troubling.

By the 1960s, enough momentum existed in the profession to deny what these ethnographers claimed, renouncing their sincere efforts as the apparent exoticizing of life elsewhere. It is a pity, then, that those dissenting intellectuals were not required in making this case to display their hands before being allowed to speak at professional meetings. For were they so required we would almost certainly find excessive amounts of soft fatty tissue of the kind that Lord Byron felt made one a real gentleman—tissue that, while proving their gentility, in no way could stand for the embodied practices of those whose lives these ethnographers claimed to know intimately. Such a test would, no doubt, tell us more about how they spent their days than would their writing. Such a test would also expose their remoteness from those very peoples who moved Marcel Mauss to write our first deep essays on the topic of how self and nonself get sorted out in other places (1935, 1938).

There is no reason to produce any inventory of attitudes about the manner in which a self can display a body-image boundary that is quite flexible, especially when such an inventory can be so readily dispelled by skeptics. However, as Boas illustrated for the Kwakiutl long ago, there is little sense in talking about persons as we might know them if the ground rules admit from the start what for outsiders seems unacceptable. Citing Boas's pioneering work, Goldman noted many such examples among the Kwakiutl, including the idea that personae can be willfully discarded when removed masks fly back to the sky world (1975:228):

—The Grizzly Bear masks and skin return home by themselves.

—Seals are surprised and seen as men before they have time to put on their masks. . . .

—On owl masks: "Owls are men, for we all have owl masks." The dead go toward their owl masks and fly about as owls. "The owl names the name of the owner of the owl mask."

—Masks become excited behind their curtain at the sound of beating and yelling at a ceremony.

Yes, these cases are all "unusual"—unusual in that they will *always* appear improbable or sensational to a skeptical rationalist, to the involuted postmod-

ernist, and to the old-fashioned psychoanalyst. They are also unusual in that—
like illness itself—they are adaptive enough so as never to present themselves
in a "usual" form. They demonstrate, in other words, instances of dissociative
projection that only achieve "normality" after the transformations for which
they are catalysts get assimilated recursively into a narrative of interconnected
events.

I will not, therefore, make any extended argument for the need to take seriously anthropology's literature on animism from Tylor onward, for this would
be to repeat arguments that have already been made.[8] Nor will I address the
defensive posture of anthropology's academic industry, especially the version
of that industry that claims some moral high ground through the kind of
rhetorical sentimentality that is our current fashion. What I will say, moreover,
has nothing to do with recent theories of the person that get drummed up in
academic high society. Instead, I will describe the damaging consequences of
normalizing the exotic, since I would not, in this forum at least, be permitted
to display my own hands as evidence of what I do on any given day.

Getting Poisoned

Getting poisoned in the field can be a good thing. It happened to me in 1981,
while studying the uses and abuses of magic in Bali. I cite the year here, because at that time our field was busy telling everyone that anthropology's earlier interest in structure and ritual had skewed the lived worlds of those we
study. Magic and ritual—the things that had fascinated our professional an-
cestors—were thought to be part of the luxurious fantasizing of both intellectual and actual colonists.

Though years later it would seem no more nor less demanding than my stays
in other Asian countries, I had initially been discouraged by professionals who
had worked in Bali from going there in the first place.[9] It was "overstudied"
and "ruined by tourism"—perhaps too soft a field site in a discipline whose
members had traditionally fascinated one another by extraordinary tales of
survival. But, for a recent philosophy graduate,[10] it was an ideal setting in
which to explore the cultural construct of the person, especially as that construct got tossed and torn in ecstatic dissociative trances. Of course, at the time
I had no idea of what I was getting into. Except for a warning from an experienced British ethnographer that my topic (by then defined as the interpretation of masks) could be dangerous, more commonly I was confronted by the
derision of fellow anthropologists who felt that studying masked ritual was a
romantic thing of the past—even potentially an elitist endeavor, since it clearly
involved things that, if they existed at all, were not part of the "everyday"
world of Balinese commoners. Never mind that some of those same anthropologists have since come to write about the impact of magical beliefs upon
those "everyday" Balinese; suffice it to say that the moment when I arrived was

important because modernity seemed to have struck the island as well as those who studied it with something like a vengeance.

As it turned out, I began my work in the usual sort of way—finding out who made masks, where they were used, how many kinds there were, how they were consecrated. All seemed important to me, but it was the last of these that provided my introduction to a world that my professional peers appeared to know nothing about; for, despite the volumes of literature on my topic, I could find no examination of the correlation between woods used for masks and what was clearly an indigenous pharmacopoeia. My "over-studied" topic, in other words, turned out—despite the many books in print about it—to contain crucial dimensions that were "never studied." Indeed, before long I realized that my inquiries were leading me deeper and deeper into a world of experience that was, indeed, *very* "exotic" and, moreover, almost wholly alien to me.

Now, you may ask at this juncture why I am telling this story, rather than, say, writing about Balinese ethnobotany. You may also ask why, as a professional anthropologist, I have never written an ethnography of an indigenous group—for the experiences that I had could for some probably be elucidating or instructive. You may ask why my Balinese experiences inform everything I write, even though I rarely write about them directly—why I have never presented my experiences as "data" to be scrutinized by others. Well, the reason I am framing these experience so narrowly is because, in fact, I am not going to describe them, to prove in some narrative form that they are "mine." Rather, what I am going to describe is how I came to see that there were certain doors of perception that were opened for me, thresholds that I had looked through but did not cross; for had I crossed them, I could not be writing what I write at this moment. I am not being coy here; I am merely pointing out that getting poisoned was a good thing for me.

It would, of course, be improper (if not perhaps dangerous) to describe in too much detail how my "initiation" occurred. But I can say that it all happened in a most unexpected way. In fact, it was probably the fault of my camera;[11] for I had taken a photo of a magical covering over a powerful mask—a photo that a god would not have allowed were I not meant to have it. In other words, there was no prohibition on approaching a magical object other than the wrath or the patronage of the inhabiting spirit. Tourists, for instance, may happily walk across a graveyard at night; but, if being in that powerful place were part of some calling, one had better be ritually prepared. On other occasions my thoroughly reliable camera had jammed under similar circumstances, so the outcome of taking such photos was, I was told, in the god's hands, not mine.

Had I known more of Bali at the time, I would surely have recognized the request for a copy of the photo by a member of a competing clan as an urgent plea to control a potentially overpowering force. But there was no way of my knowing that capturing an image on film could be construed as a power move of its own kind. Moreover, there were several other signals that I will not describe; but suffice it to say that my professional loneliness had led me to spending long days deciphering in my appalling German Wolfgang Weck's 1937 *Heilkunde und Volkstum auf Bali* (*Curing and Folk Wisdom on Bali*). The book intrigued me not only because of the fact that Weck was himself a medical doctor (a profession I had once intended to follow), but because, unlike most of the ethnographies I had read, what Weck said rang true to me. As I read what he wrote about magical attacks, I began to realize that I was myself in the midst of one.

So, when the day came that I was offered datura (brugmansia) in a traditional Balinese dish, I accepted the food politely, but disposed of it when I removed myself to dine. When a servant later appeared that day to inquire how I was doing in the hospital, he was more than surprised to learn that I was in excellent health and only curious about why he should ask such a question. What he had anticipated was that sufficient poisoning would, were it not fatal, at least leave me in a restless panic, the outcome of which would be a state of memory-less anxiety—a psychotic fear of each waking moment that eventually would leave me spending long, listless days in a zombie-like state.

Why, then, do I call my experience a poisoning rather than an "attempted" poisoning? Because my survival made it clear to everyone familiar with the incident that my identity had been permanently changed by the experience. I had been, as it were, inoculated by a god's protective efforts. There was no other explanation for my survival. Now, for whatever reasons, I have been spared to tell a story, and that story is about transcendence.

The Essential Fear

I remember the moment well. It was June 1977. I was wearing my Oxford gown and sitting in the University Schools with a neatly printed examination book containing questions that would determine whether my year had been usefully spent. Some hours later, I reached the final page of the exam and found a question that made me laugh almost openly. Perhaps it was the nearly six hours already spent clutching a pen; perhaps it was the formality of the experience. But for whatever reason, I was brought up short by a question that asked me to comment on British cultural traits.

Because students were required to choose from a list of possible essay topics, I put this question aside and only recalled it that afternoon when we cracked the traditional bottles of champagne as we spewed into High Street following the completion of our exams. To my surprise, a number of my classmates had elected to answer this question, and it soon became clear to me that what I thought to be a humorous example of the "essentializing" of other cultures was for many a serious and legitimate inquiry. If there were, indeed, autonomous and potentially incommensurate ways of embodying experience, then did it not follow that some cultures would excel at certain domains of experience and knowledge? And if a collectivity can develop certain excellences, did it not then also follow that not all such social collectivities would excel in the same sorts of ways?

This basic idea—which, by the way, is also evident in a much more politically correct discourse on multiculturalism—comes dangerously close to openly racist discourse because its logic necessitates certain conclusions that are as unpalatable as they are morally suspect. Indeed, it was a small step from saying that specific modes of thinking develop unique techniques for experiencing the world to saying that some would be better than others for specific tasks. To call one thing "better" is to have established a hierarchy, and to have done that is to have set off down the bumpy road of social Darwinism and, equally troubling, of eugenic programming. What, after all, do we mean at the social level when we believe biologically that the "fittest" survive, or when embryos or sperm are selected for the version of humanness they are meant to reproduce? "If you can't stand the heat," Richard Nixon used to love saying, "get out of the kitchen": it is the same idea. If you have not got what it takes, you will never be one of the few good men that the Marines are always in search of.

Without revisiting the history of "planned parenthood" from Herbert Spencer to Julian Huxley, it is clear that there is no diversity to "honor" if there is no difference; and if there is *relative* difference, then there is choice. If there is preference, then there is hierarchy. As soon as we have hierarchy, alas, we have inequality—unless, as Phillips (1994:79) points out, we are prepared to argue that a boxer's view of a psychoanalytic session is as insightful as a psychiatrist's view of boxing.

Though, indeed, the boxer may sometimes have the advantage of his own insights, our lists of psychiatrists holding down important institutional posts is enough evidence in itself to show that our love of novelty hardly matches our cultural obsession with achieved status—that is, of social hierarchy. Otherwise, we would see no problem in having the psychiatrist devote her days to boxing as might the boxer to the analytical couch. In fact, though the novelty of either may endear us to a boxing psychiatrist or an analyzing boxer, our love of that novelty is hardly adequate to sustain the belief that those two worlds are anything like equal. If, in other words, one manages to swallow the notion that relative difference can be maintained without preference (that is, without one thing being "better" than another), then one need only ask why so many academic professionals who preach diversity from the pulpit are wholly reticent of living at all outside of the institutional networks that sustain them. I think here especially of my socialist colleagues who, in spite of their politics, still send their children to Oxford and Harvard—which, of course, brings us right back to having a better look at those hands before such gentlemen start their engines and we, in turn, express our hope that the best man wins.

Though historical examples are less discomforting because they are, by their distance, so easily dismissed, the process of stereotyping continues unchecked in a society in which achieved status reigns above all else. In this respect, America will never solve the ongoing oppression of its so-called minorities, because the presence of some minority is required to create a relative hierarchy of achievement in which heroes distinguish themselves from those less fortunate Others. The problem, in other words, with focusing on the everyday, or workaday, experiences of commoners is that our doing so itself creates a hierarchy in which *we* become the voice for *them*. In America, to salt the wound, we then hide our hierarchies within a rhetoric of equality. Show me the university professor who has no interest in working under the "bright lights" and I will show you either a professional second-class citizen or what his colleagues would consider a damned fool.

Yet I know for a fact that I will never learn to speak a new language as well as a five-year-old native speaker. I know that I will never learn to ski as effortlessly as my son who grew up skiing. Likewise, I know that I can never fully appreciate the famine of an Ethiopian by watching television or, indeed, know his or her hunger by visiting a refugee encampment. I can no better survive Saharan heat than a Bedoin can sense the presence of a whale beneath an ocean swell. The problem is that acknowledging these things so easily leads to views of the Other that are totally problematic, because for most of us it is but a short leap from "kids make good skiers" to "mountain dwellers make good skiers" to "Austrians make good skiers." And it is yet another small leap that can then lead us to even more problematic perceptions of Others, like the often-voiced racist stereotype that blacks make better athletes. Do Eskimos sense more variations in weather? Do Japanese excel at collective endeavors? Here in Vermont, for instance, one can on most days hear political lobbyists arguing for special visas for low-cost Jamaican apple pickers on the grounds that they possess the inherent ability to handle fruit delicately—as if they somehow have a genetic disposition to this form of manual labor. Where do experiential considerations, in other words, give way to national, racial, and ethnic biases? And how are statistical generalities used to destroy real difference? Hitler did very well at this—for example, noting the numbers of Jews who were academic achievers or numbers of unwed Catholic mothers—but so, unfortunately, did recent uses of the bell curve.[12]

The problem, in other words, with essentializing shared experiences is that there is no lack of quantitative evidence to support almost any sort of conclusion, but the logical conclusions to which such essentializing draws us are nearly always both morally and democratically wrong. In extreme cases of such stereotyping (what we now call "profiling"), the tendency to adopt racially driven views of others leads to highly offensive assumptions. If Muslim terrorists only train other Muslims for acts of terror, people will always assume that such terrorists are Muslim, because generalizations are based on generalities that, in turn, are based on the repeated verification of those same assumptions. We employ, in other words, many kinds of shorthand just to get through a day, even if that very generalizing process so often leads to quite sloppy and morally inappropriate thinking. Only when our stereotypes are overturned before us through personal encounters, or when we can distance ourselves from them over time, do they actually stand out as wholly unacceptable.

So, this idea—that various culturally embedded forms of knowledge will be better suited to particular life-forms—per force places the notion of modes of thought in enough of a potentially bad light to make most of us uncomfortable about saying much of anything about the ways in which culture conditions values. At the same time, as long ago as Plato the idea was widely recognized that the character of our social institutions would be reflected in collectively valued notions of what makes us human. Aristotle's similar belief that "what makes the world one will also be what makes a person" is conditioned by like notions about how the human body and, say, a governmental body are more than metaphorically related. Why else, for instance, did Americans continue to "give blood for America" long after the September 11 hijackings? Why else do we describe terrorist organizations as "cells" and their behavior as "viral"? Why else were American news broadcasters so obsessed with reciting the word "anthrax" when so many more dangerous threats were being faced by Americans both at home and abroad? Clearly, a horrendous crisis was causing us to reify the connection between the self and that social body called "our culture."

Because we both take offense in, and recognize the social currency of, such assumptions, we also feel a natural urge to police them in ways that are sometimes appropriate and sometimes not. Either way, the fact of the matter is that if you think of the self as a negotiated terrain of host-pathogen balancing, you will by definition be less concerned about the presence of a little Otherness in your life. All French people, for instance, may not share the view that Americans are too antiseptic about the body, but it is a view that we nonetheless—and with some accuracy—call "French."

So why continue to talk about cultural variation if it always leads either to stereotypical "profiling" or to the covert deployment of some hierarchy within a rhetoric of equality? And does it really matter that the French possess a culturally driven notion of the self that sees individuals as made up in part of difference?

The answer to the first of these questions is that Hegel was right about the need for Other in defining the self, even if he was wrong about this relationship always being militant. And the answer to the second of these questions is, well, yes.

Transformation "c'est la moi"

In her popular account of the variations in health-care practices in France, Germany, the United Kingdom, and the United States, the late Lynn Payer described the importance in French society of thinking of the body as *la terrain*— a concept that has no easy English equivalent, but essentially one that encapsulates a cultural predilection for recognizing a disease as not only an invasion from outside, but as the combination of outside influences and the body's reaction to those influences. In this view, morbidity is not just a function of what pathogens do to us, but also of how successfully or unsuccessfully that Outsider is assimilated—"a combination of some type of outside insult and the body's reaction to that insult" (61).

As a consequence of this view, French doctors by and large "are more likely to try to find ways to modify the reaction as well as fight off the insult," whereas the health-care practices of certain other Western nations tend to focus more on destroying completely the insult itself. French medicine, then, is more accommodating, more homeopathic, and more attuned to health-related therapies that strengthen and condition the body. The French—as is evidenced in certain of their recent national health policies—feel that paying for baths and spas might be an important part of health care, the concrete outcome of which is not only evidenced in the French tendency to see clinical health as a function of well-being in some broad sense, but apparent in such an equal distribution of health benefits that the WHO recently rated France number one in health care worldwide. Yes, there are French researchers just as adamant about eliminating HIV or malaria as their colleagues elsewhere, but there is actually as deeply embedded in France a cultural discourse about recognizing and assimilating the outside as there is about eliminating it. Vaccinology (the *assimilation* of pathogens) is an acknowledged theoretical domain in France, whereas in America (where pathogens are *eliminated* immunologically), the discipline only has meaning in a strictly scientific sense. In the United States, we do not, in other words, talk about exposing ourselves to pathogens in the same way that we describe the need to fortify our immune systems. Try raising the subject of vaccinology at your next cocktail party and you will be dutifully impressed by the silence and vacant stares you have visited upon yourself.

What, then, might we make, Payer asks, of the cultural idea of the French as a people tolerant of "a little bit of dirt"? If we look at the numbers of French doctors who are licensed homeopaths or at the research on plasmodistatic drugs—that is, drugs that alter a body's response to plasmodia (the agents of malaria) rather than killing pathogens outright—the answer must be "a good bit." Are the French, then, likely to be better at addressing the problems of how the world might deal with the multiresistant bacteria that have grown out of our overuse of antibiotics designed to eliminate the Outside? The answer is, yes, of course. And if we, then, say that the French are more likely to succeed intellectually in balancing antibodies and antigens than are their American colleagues who are dead set on killing off those antigens, are we not also, then, saying that stereotypes about French bathing habits are "real" enough to be evidenced in their scientific research programs?

So what, one might ask, makes attending to this stereotype any more productive than the stereotypes that may as readily be constructed for other cultural groups? The answer here is easy: because the French assimilative treatment of biological (and cultural) differences creates a kind of transformational environment that is ideologically more creative than is, say, the cathartic relational model with which Americans are by and large more comfortable. The assimilative value of *la terrain*, in other words, itself stands as an indicator of some shared confidence about how a productive encounter with Other (be it real or imagined) may be orchestrated. To put it differently, in acknowledging that the self is in part Other, we force ourselves also to acknowledge that social encounters only produce positive outcomes when their dynamic nature is attended to. As Ricoeur says of his own book title, "*Oneself as Another* [Soi-même comme un autre] suggests from the outset that the selfhood of oneself implies otherness to such an intimate degree that one cannot be thought of without the other, that instead one passes into the other, as we might say in Hegelian terms" (1992:3). Implicit, then, in this notion of the self is a thing that is dynamic and, in fact, sufficiently dynamic that it cannot exist without acknowledging the formative importance of its ontological, its narrative, and above all its social Others. This interdependence, after all, is what has largely distinguished Continental phenomenology from the empirical focus of British-American philosophy for nearly a century. Moreover, it is also why English-speaking ("American") anthropologists regularly confuse the term "phenomenological" with the term "phenomenal"; for the former grows out of a particular sociohistorical argument about the *embedded* nature of human identity while the latter implies more generally that we consider human identity as a thing made meaningful through its sensory and its experiential manifestations. The difference may seem subtle, but it is also crucial.

Once acknowledged, however, this discrimination makes it much easier to understand why anthropological examples of Others' modes of thought are so compelling, and why, by contrast, we appear so parochial when we normalize the "everyday" worlds of Others—when we mistake, that is, the "phenomenal" for the "phenomenological." For, in the latter of these, we are not merely trying to say that other cultures have essential features that we may not have. Quite the contrary: we are saying that other modes of thought that define the self through its capacity to assimilate *always* offer more creative versions of how one grows and is transformed through social encounters than do those notions of self that survive by eliminating the outside. Indeed, by this simple discrimination one can nearly measure the confidence of any social group about the sovereignty of its borders and, at the same time, produce an inventory of cultural settings in which self and other differ dramatically from the version we today see in, say, "magic bullet" medicine or in "precision bombing."

This assimilative notion of a body's terrain is, thus, more important than it may at first appear because it has its own built-in mechanism for revising stereotypes. In allowing for productive mutations, *la terrain* distinguishes itself from a cathartic model of self that expels difference from what phenomenologists refer to as its regional ontology—in this case, its body-image boundary. It is not at all difficult then to see how a notion of selfhood based on the elimination of difference will be much more likely to reify stereotypes of the Other and, by extension, to promote an incommensurable relationship between "the self and its behavioral world," to recall Hallowell (1955). In recognizing and eliminating nonself (that is, in immunology), little stimulus exists for interaction, because the goal of interacting is to neutralize Otherness. Is it any wonder then that ethnic minorities who grow up abroad have so frequently voiced the opinion that they never feel so much the alienation of being a minority than upon returning to the United States—even, I might add, upon returning from countries better known than America for their racism?

I have, in other words, used French popular "culture" as an example here— rather than, for example, something ethnographically "exotic"—because it would clearly be wrong to claim that the mere act of noting a proliferation of homeopaths in France is itself an act of exoticizing difference. Nor am I choosing this example because I would want anyone to think that all people with French passports value *la terrain*. The reason this concept is noted is because an awareness of *la terrain* encourages a tendency toward *assimilation*, which is different than a tendency toward *elimination*.[13] Likewise, the famous examples that I described in the first part of this chapter were also chosen for their assimilative capacities, for their articulation of the complexities of human interaction as a baseline condition rather than as a thing thought up after modernism. They are not, in other words, unusual examples called up only to incite the suspicion of postmodernists!

The problem then with neutralizing difference by eliminating it or even by reducing it to a subset of the normal is that the outcome of this endeavor is much more damaging than might at first appear to be the case; for, in ruling out the thrill of the unknown, we also rule out any prospect for creative mutation. To put it another way, if the other that one engages is believed only to be a reflexive extension of an isolated self, there can, by definition, be no mutual transformation. If there is no social and reciprocal abandonment of an authoritarian self, there can be no changing of anything; if there is no risk of self-loss, there is also no catalyst for growth.

"Honk If I'm Polish"; or, A Selfish Argument for Abandoning
Postmodernism

Thus far in this chapter I have used the notion of culture as a broad rubric for
the assumed collectivities of which individuals (rightly or wrongly) consider
themselves to be a part, or against which they define themselves as outsiders.
In so doing, I have steered clear of the debate over whether one can rightly
speak at all of the identity of a group of others or of the identity that any self
may assume others to share. The onset of reflexive ideas in social anthropology introduced a near complete ban on speaking or writing about collectivities, even those produced as the imaginative constructs, or even as the fantasies,
of a lucid ego. So, permit me now to outline my reasons for framing my discussion in ways that have openly ignored postmodernism, and in so doing to
illustrate why I have here and elsewhere characterized postmodern theory as
ideologically reactionary.

THE POSTMODERN VIEW OF SELF IS NOT ASTRUCTURAL, BUT ANTISTRUCTURAL

In anthropology, one of the greatest weaknesses of the postmodern view of self
is its assumption that structuralism ossifies or ignores the phenomenal domain
of individual experience. Though, as we have seen, Durkheim may certainly
have pointed us in that direction by banning individual psychology from the
examination of collective ideology, what he almost certainly understood as the
function of social categories was rather different from how we now view them
in hindsight. In fact, there is even a postmodern view of Durkhein that ac-
knowledges the need to assess him less dogmatically (Meštrović 1992). Without
discussing this at length, one must understand here that Durkheim's quibble
with psychology was in large measure the result of his belief that the examination of modes of thought could go forward in safety only so long as we restricted our inquiry to collective interactions among those who shared domains
of language and thought. As long as we were not examining how those categories were judged psychologically by individual actors, we need not attach
value to—or, in so doing, state a hierarchical preference for—one system over
another. Whether we call these domains cultural categories or experiential
tropes mattered less than the fact that culture was constituted of broadly
shared metaphors within which were embedded the explanatory networks that
allowed for human agreement.

Metaphors do demonstrably convey viscerally shared, and often covert,
ways of organizing experience.[14] This is not difficult to demonstrate, but it
does require a certain critical distance from the white noise of the local networks we are attuned to. One only has to see how metaphors mutate in what
used to be called "traditional" societies—that is, to experience having been

poisoned—to understand why the structural straw man of postmodernism gets torched each year at Burning Man.

Looked at bluntly, nobody ever said that cultures were fixed and immutable, except perhaps for a few postmodernists who have not the courage to be moved by genuine difference. Instead, they use the word "exotic" to describe everything that is potentially different—which, of course, is necessary if one is petrified about being changed by encounters with the unknown. In this sense, postmodernism is highly dilettantish, because if one is a smart-enough dresser (or under-dresser), it is possible to ward off challenges to one's identity by flirting in professional settings with artificial danger.

POSTMODERNISTS ARE NOT SELFISH ENOUGH

The postmodernist is scared by the possibility of losing the fragile professional edifice he has worked so hard to construct, in part because the indeterminacy of postmodernism creates uncertainty that itself leads to personal insecurity and a lack of conviction. So, when he looks locally, the postmodernist wants us to concentrate on each private neologism that gives what he says a novel appearance. At the same time, he cannot structure his sensations because he is antistructuralist.

Because he lacks local empathic order, he must project his sensitivities globally. Postmodernists, therefore, talk about very *big* things much of the time because the smaller things do not really interest them—unless, of course, they can reflexively gain favorable interest on their otherwise deep feelings of neglect by glamorizing local things with invented, Latin-like words. Whether they do not openly want to be wanted I cannot say. What I can say is that they need some coaching. Touching oneself is a start; but being touched by another is much better because it not only informs you intimately about the lived world of the person touching you, but it also invites you to acknowledge how touch itself is a vehicle for empathic transference.

Prejudicing the intellect, furthermore, severely skews our ability to sense how shared domains of understanding get creatively manipulated in group rites, because such prejudicing limits our awareness of how each of our senses contributes its own unique forms of social awareness. Occasionally someone is able to sneak such an idea into print (I am thinking especially of Stoller's work on taste [1989, 1997]);[15] more often our academic inquisitionists prohibit such considerations from seeing the light of day. A "taste" of what I am referring to may be read online (where peer reviews do not silence the unusual), though unmonitored talk has a tendency to get "out of hand," as we say. At the same time, simply enjoying oneself makes an excellent beginning.

POSTMODERNISTS LIKE PSYCHOANALYSIS (AND NOT JUST LACAN)

No one ever said that traditions are static, except for those who have never been transformed by collective catharsis. But postmodernists for the most part like psychoanalysis because it pledges to offer developmental stability, and it privileges a version of individuality with which Westerners are most familiar.[16] One reason why postmodernists fail to recognize the flexibility of the self in traditional life is because the word "tradition" also connotes stability. If you spend too much time reading, and not enough time running naked, you will surely believe that stability is a "static" idea that you may not know at all, but that (whatever it may be) cannot be what you wish you could become—for becoming *should* be destabilizing.

The problem here stems from never having dirtied oneself in any group rite. If, in fact, one had done so, it would become immediately apparent that meaningful transformation has nothing to do with navel-gazing, and probably nothing much to do with a Protestant-Buddhist nonself too. This is why the *structure* of change worldwide is so stable—that is, why most "premodern" peoples have not jettisoned the idea that rites of passage affect people profoundly. Psychological instability is ameliorated by structural stability because change is a very dangerous thing. People do not become better integrated by thinking about being different. They become better integrated by laying down their modern and postmodern firearms and allowing themselves to dissociate in the presence of another human being. Van Gennep realized this in 1909. We just have not bothered to read him. Nor have we bothered to recognize that ritual is, for those immersed within it, anything but the repetitive domain that laboratory behaviorists would have us think.

Humans do not get transformed through psychotherapy; they get transformed through selective dissociation. You do not, that is, get healed of your obsession with the self by becoming more obsessed with the self. Postmodernism has things very wrong here, and the evidence is made even clearer by what postmodernism takes to be distinctive about contemporary life.

POSTMODERNISTS COVERTLY (AND SOMETIMES OVERTLY) BELIEVE IN EVOLUTION

Modernism is a reaction to tradition, and postmodernism is, as its name indicates, a reaction to modernism. Being reactionary, it requires some faith in historical continuity—in the evolving nature of social change. The world of postmodernism is not, in other words, the nonsense world of dadaism, but the surrealist's world of psychological novelty. Though it may claim to be ahistorical, its "newness" is necessarily measured against what it is meant to replace. I have never heard a postmodernist say that his or her ideas were old and unimportant.

If postmodernists cannot assure themselves that life has evolved from states of continuity to those of discontinuity (from determinacy to indeterminacy, from dull order to cute chaos), they cannot offer any new higher-order theory about why things today just seem so jumbled up all the time. But whoever said that the living of life was anything other than chaotic? Where are all of the voices from the past that show life to have once been only dull and unexciting? Well, I can tell you where they are. They are in the postmodern novel itself, which is perhaps the only place I know where ennui is elevated to a major virtue.

But at the level of collective ideas, there can be no such thing as evolutionary continuity. The word "culture" becomes more or less important depending on the human need for identifying with others. When times are flush, we allow ourselves to believe that our lives are controlled by how far we can network worldwide as a metaphorical McDonald's hamburger. And in the security of our homes, we feel good about feeling alone. We even write books about our alienation from the warmth of our institutional offices[17] or as Pollock (1996) has cleverly shown, from the halls of our professional schools where the lament over a loss of traditional authority gets reconstructed into self-indulged heroic epic. We even believe that culture has been replaced by a global order, only to find that in moments of crisis we rush home to touch up the paint on the fading coats of arms that have been relegated to the closets of virtual neglect.

Moments of *instability* do induce interdependence, which is why historically we find culture most dynamically articulated in instances such as those claimed by postmodernists to be uniquely new. This is not to say that there is nothing new, but that in the words of Lemert's book title (1997), "postmodernism is not what you think." What Lemert means by this is that if postmodernism exists at all, it is not about the act of thinking, but about other things that we do today. However, because postmodernism is also a narrative "about the extent to which the world has changed" (53), it requires some deeper acceptance that something like a "real" world has existed. This is the way in which postmodernism sees itself as radical, as Baudrillard's "hyperreality in which simulation of reality is more real than the thing itself" (27)—where "Disneyworld replications of a mythical America are the real American thing—more real than any actual American village" (28).[18] Without begging the question of just what "radical" can mean here, it is clear that whatever is going on, there are some big claims being made about earlier times that can evoke Poussin's images of Arcadia, or Rousseau's noble savage, as much as Mickey Mouse and Ronald McDonald.

Of course, the attraction of believing in social evolution is that there must have at one time been groups of people who were less self-consciously aware of the possibility of once having been less aware. But to think that this "newness" is evidenced in the unique mutability of contemporary life—in the trope by which a presumably less mutable life has now become mutable—is simply, as Lemert illustrates, wrongheaded. Though time does create unique notions of what has happened, or is happening, around us, culture was probably no more immutable in the past than it is today—even if anthropologists have been traditionally attracted to domains where apparent stasis allows for the more easy management of one's own presumptions. Psychologically, of course, other societies may well have been, if anything, more mutable in terms of identity change than we are today. Ancient Greeks, modern Balinese, and even at times "enlightened" Europeans have all displayed global and transnational tendencies,[19] even if the more physically mobile reality of life today means that these events take place with greater frequency than before. Culture is, in this line of thinking, "always *in motion*—becoming, reproducing itself even when disintegrating at the 'core' and transforming, in a constant ebb and flow. . . . as a result of the dialectic between internal developments, global and other external forces, and social agents, who are almost always cosmopolitan" (Ohnuki-Tierney 2001:244). For the very notion of a culture as something hermetic is predicated upon the assumption that "there once were cultures, each boxed in a territorial unit, whose territorial boundaries suddenly burst open" (242), and that these changes are by and large the outcome of the new global order. So, aside from the deeply disappointing idea that our own era may lack the importance we wish for it, what makes today different? To answer this question we must make one additional claim about self and other in postmodernity.

POSTMODERNISTS ADVANCE AS TRUTH A VIEW OF WORLD CHANGE THAT CANNOT BE SUSTAINED

In a popular account of what he takes to be American hypocrisy, Shapiro (1994) lists page after page of the disjunction between what Americans believe of themselves and the world and what research shows, in fact, to be the case. Americans are number one in percentage of students who say they are good in math, but last in the percentage of student who actually are good in math (64). We are number one in the percentage of people who believe it is necessary to be able to read a map, and number one in ignorance of geography among young people (68). We are number one in membership in human rights groups, and number one in not ratifying international human rights treaties (114). We are number one in percentage of population that believes that the commandment "Thou shalt not steal" still applies today, and number one in robberies and thieves per capita (132). The lists offered by Shapiro actually fill an entire paperback, but the above-cited examples are sufficient to paint a picture of a modern world whose professed values are very much at odds with the actual behavior of its citizenry.

Now, the most common postmodern explanation claims that the flow of people, of images, and of resources in the contemporary era creates a kind of "creole" world where West Africans now make printed kente cloth baseball caps because Koreans in New Jersey printed cheap versions of the first African caps made of high quality woven kente cloth. Why baseball caps? Because once African Americans had exploited the use of kente strips as college-graduation attire, few marketing options remained for Ghanaian merchants eager to sell ethnicity to African American customers, and everyone in America (and now around the world) wants to wear a baseball cap—even American football players. Here, the cosmopolitan flow of images and practices defies any kind of traditional cultural attribution. Balinese make African sculpture for sale to Westerners and then themselves collect their imitations in imitation of those who buy their imitations. In such settings it becomes all but necessary to reject the idea that these artifacts are the outcome of hermetic practices in fixed locations; rather, they devolve from practices that by any definition are borderless.

However, as Harvey points out, "the shifting social construction of space and time creates severe problems of identity: To what space do I as an individual belong? Do I express my idea of citizenship in my neighborhood, city, region, nation, or world? These are the sorts of questions that are being at least partially addressed within the postmodern rhetoric, even when the answers (the passive acceptance of fragmentation, for example) are patently false" (1991:77). For socialists, Harvey included, these conditions are created by the endless search for profit and the geographic mobility on which the practices of flight capitalists thrive. Part of the "flexibility" that results has been understood, from Gramsci onward, as a function of what sociologists see as the classical disjunction between normative and emergent domains of experience. In this view, not only social life but also individual identity is enough uprooted from its setting to make possible—even to encourage—an emergent set of values that are much removed from, and even contradict, other coextensively held principles. Hindus in India wear leather jackets against naked chests in home-grown gangster movies, even though they are prohibited by caste to associate with such polluted substances; and they keeps pets and go to restaurants with roughly equal degrees of uneasiness and enthusiasm.

In such a world, it is argued, the only way that the contradictions existing between normative and emergent values can be justified is by flexible identities that enable the postmodern individual to inhabit diverse spaces (for example, Martin 1994). When you are at home, you are Korean; when at work, a capitalist; when travelling locally, an American; when abroad, a tourist, a cultural ambassador, an ethnographer, and so on. This is the reality that writers such as Appadurai (1996) and Gupta and Ferguson (1992, 1997a, 1997b) have explored so insightfully.

But is the apparent chaos and rapidity of contemporary life the symptom of postmodernity or merely the sign of something else? No one would argue that the disjunctions are not there; but if they have as profound an effect on each of us as those who write about postmodernity claim, then we, least of all, are in any position to possess or to use the intellectual skills necessary to explain them. Fortunately, however, such disjunctions also existed abundantly in the past, and still continue to occur in noncosmopolitan settings worldwide; it is only, I would argue, that we now seem so determined to ignore the easy solutions to settling our anxieties about the act of exploring what can and cannot be known. This unwillingness is, perhaps, the most insidious feature of the so-called postmodern condition—insidious because its remedy is as obvious as it is unacknowledged; obvious because it is, well, age old. It merely awaits reinvention—awaits an awakening, that is, in a new, more pleasurable form.

"Lived Worlds" of the Living Dead

As a student of phenomenology in the early 1970s it was my habit to spend my one-month spring break each year in Spain. The sunny, arid climate could not have been more different from the gray dampness of Belgium. Moreover, at that time it was so inexpensive that getting there and staying for the month was actually less costly than sitting in my college rooms in Leuven. In fact, I would set off for the train station with my student travel card and little more than $100; usually I would return weeks later, perhaps a bit thinner than when I left, with some spare change still in pocket.

On the first such trip, I was accompanied by a friend with whom I split rooming costs. Upon reaching Madrid, we decided one evening to take in a movie. Scanning the newspaper, he noticed that the cult American film "Night of the Living Dead" was playing in one of the suburban theaters. It would take some doing to get there, but he really wanted to see the film, and I had more than a passing interest in it.

You see, as a Pittsburgh native, one couldn't help but know of it. Before becoming a cult film, it had played for years as the last film of the night at many neighborhood drive-in theaters. I also had other reasons for wanting to see it myself, the principal one being that it had been made by the boyfriend of a good friend's sister. Though neither my high-school buddy nor I had much use for his older sister or her friends, when it came time for soliciting bodies for the zombie scenes all of my friends volunteered. Ironically, neither my best friend nor I were among the stand-ins. His mom had insisted that he pay his own way since the age of sixteen, which meant he had to work late nights and most weekends at the local dairy, and my parents had insisted that the best way to grow up involved working whenever possible. When I was not delivering papers (starting as a seven-year-old) or working at loading and unloading trucks of unpleasant chemicals at my father's water purification company, I was usually saddled with housepainting, lawn mowing, and whatever else needed to be done on weekends. So now, years later in Madrid, I would finally get to see my friends on film.

I suppose this event may have qualified as an early precursor to what today would be labeled a postmodern experience. Seconds after the film began, it became clear to me that it had not been subtitled. Rather, I soon realized, I would be treated to seeing my old high-school buddies walking through the fields not far from our hometown speaking the most lovely Castilian Spanish. To make matters funnier still, we were all of us very bad students of Spanish in high school, because none of us was terribly focused academically then, and everyone knew that Spanish was the easiest way to fulfill our school's language requirement. I can still hear one of my classmates answering a question posed to him in Spanish with the words, "No lo understando." To hear friends speaking in dubbed voices was odd enough; to hear them speaking as native speakers in a movie about western Pennsylvania was truly weird.

For some time after this event, I could not quite come to terms with what I had experienced. After all, despite the film's cheap budget—or rather because of it—the superficial manipulation of the "real" world made, if anything, a more disturbing scene than anything out of Hollywood. Included in the drama were not only my friends who shuffled around our local fields past the "Vacuform" spiders that had been placed on the sides of trees to enhance the viewer's uneasiness, but there were also the local news announcers and other celebrities I had grown up with all speaking to one another in the finest Spanish about the munching of plastic body parts by the crazed zombies that my friends were impersonating.

And all of this was happening in the midst of the final days our first TV war—the broadcasting of the tragic events of Vietnam that had preoccupied this very group of friends. As one of the lucky ones, I was now studying abroad as a college student. But my buddies had more difficult choices because they came from families that basically assumed that after you were out of high school, you were on your own. Of the guys I associated with after school and at work, one was a quiet Korean American who was way too serious—he did five tours of duty; one was my pool-sharking partner, who came back addicted to heroin; one went to Canada; one joined the Peace Corps; one ended up in an asylum, and on and on. The list could run to pages, but seeing my friends transformed into proper Spanish zombies in a cheap local movie that was an actual part of our daily living at the time made the notion of hyperreality seem trivial many years before the idea of postmodernism ever entered anthropological discourse. Knowing how heavily Vietnam had weighed on the hearts of those now-Castilian zombies made me come to wonder of which foreign war my friends were now true veterans.

I raise this episode then not only because it could so easily be construed as a "lived experience" of the postmodern sort, but also because watching this classic horror film again, I am moved by just how compressed time becomes in moments of deep psychological stress as well as how the noncommittal nature of the flexible postmodern identity is further deadened by the zombie-like responses of immature or atrophied senses. Why, I also wondered, were so many postmodern anxieties related to the viral-like invasion of alien personae, as if somehow we were stuck as a society in the middle of some rite of passage—stuck, that is, exactly at the transformational moment when the old person is being bid farewell, but the new one has yet to identify itself fully?[20] Why too, I wondered, was our dominant form of possession not that of love—of merging and being creatively changed through the assimilation of another enhancing life force—but of finding oneself the object of a hostile takeover that left no room for subtlety? Why were our dominant forms of possession so much more like those of psychosis and multiple personality disorder than like the assimilative possession of love in which irony makes possible the "play" of difference?[21]

Was it inevitable that our neglecting of the senses should leave us with only the radical forms of difference to accept? Could it be possible that we would only then view genuine Others as we had our own internal others—as, for example, when Native Americans (alas, even in films made by Native Americans) become characterized as either noble anachronisms or as savage reactionaries (Edgerton 1994)? And did the absence of any genuine structure to our stresses mean that we would almost never recognize that anxieties could be life-enhancing? Did the absence of collective rites, in other words, lead us to think that stress could only be negative—where the stimulus for engaging Other is replaced by our seeing Otherness in only its most extreme and threatening forms?

These are the kinds of questions that come to me time and again, as if we could only allow ourselves to assimilate the stresses that the Other causes—to use our senses to change and grow on account of the presence of that now-assimilated different thing. Was it then our avulsion of the senses and of our unwillingness to *structure* them in the subtle and uncertain space between Self and Other that made us so reticent about risking real change? Worse still, was it our lack of any collective management of stress (our lack of transformational rites) that deluded us into thinking that we actually are the inhabitants of a rapidly changing world? Maybe we all were actually now possessed, but possessed by a delusion in which we saw our world as moving quickly rather than as fading slowly from its center.

"Amodernity": The Person Reanimated

> *"Hollywood couldn't have done it better."*
>
> —*Response of an American hostage of the Taliban to the behavior of her liberators*

In his provocative early study of television, the one-time advertising executive Jerry Mander notes the consistency in "the terms people used in ordinary conversation to describe how they felt about television" (1978:157). Citing the fif-

teen phrases he most frequently recorded, he asks the reader to think obser-
vantly in ways, in fact, that we might call anthropological (157–58):

If you could somehow drop all preconception of television and read this list as though
people were describing some instrument you'd never seen yourself, I think the picture
you would obtain is of a machine that invades, controls, and deadens the people who
view it. It is not unlike the alien-operated "influencing machine" of the psychopathic
fantasy.

1) "I feel hypnotized when I watch television."
2) "Television sucks my energy."
3) "I feel like it's brainwashing me."
4) "I feel like a vegetable when I'm stuck there at the tube."
5) "Television spaces me out."
6) "Television is an addiction and I'm an addict."
7) "My kids look like zombies when they're watching."
8) "TV is destroying my mind."
9) "My kids walk around like they're in a dream because of it."
10) "Television is making people stupid."
11) "Television is turning my mind to mush."
12) "If a television is on, I just can't keep my eyes off it."
13) "I feel mesmerized by it."
14) "TV is colonizing my brain."
15) "How can I get my kids off it and back into life?"

After noting how his own son claimed that the television "makes me watch it"
(158), Mander characterized his own reaction as "antilife":

as though I'd been drained in some way, or I'd been used. I came away feeling a kind
of internal deadening, as if my whole physical being had gone dormant, the victim
of a vague soft assault. The longer I'd watch, the worse I'd feel. Afterward, there was
nearly always the desire to go outdoors or go to sleep, to recover my strength and my
feelings. Another thing. After watching television, I'd always be aware of a kind of
glowing inside my head: the images! They'd remain in there even after the set was off,
like an aftertaste. Against my will, I'd find them returning to my awareness hours
later. (159)

In part, I have quoted these passages at length because they are so familiar, so
often said, so much of the corpus of what contemporary theorists feel sepa-
rates the modern person from an earlier one who routinely spent time with
others in verbal, social, and physical intercourse. But I also quote this passage
because the author, uniquely I think, records the feelings of others in terms
they chose and then himself characterizes this ethnographic data as not just
surreal, but as "antilife"—of the lived experience, if you will, of our Castilian
zombies.

"After a while," he concludes,

I came to realize that people were describing concrete physical symptoms that neither
they nor anyone else actually believed were real. The people who would tell me that television was controlling their minds would then laugh about it. Or they would say they
were addicted to it, or felt like vegetables while watching, and then they'd laugh at that.

People were saying they were being hypnotized, controlled, drugged, deadened, but they would not assign validity to their own experience. (159–60)

For Mander, in other words, the effects of television were less that people thought that Disney World America was more real than the America they inhabited, but that the experience was characterized by concrete descriptions to which individuals assigned no validity—an activity, we might add, that otherwise is associated with life on stage: a reality TV for thespian zombies.

As we well know, various explanations that account for this confusion exist, all of which claim that modern life is chaotic and that chaos is disturbing. The modernist view, as we have noted, argues that this unstable outcome is the result of a disjunction between normative and emergent domains of experience—that people become more uncertain about what they are doing, or why they are doing what they do, in any period of human history when their expectations of change are not validated or when that validation leads to contradicting principles. The faster history unfolds, the more confused we get. The wider the gap between normative—literally that which can be "measured"—and emergent—that which is in flux—the more things appear to be changing, even when they actually become more static. Likewise, socialists argue that the rapidity of postmodern life fuels networks of power by which it becomes wholly possible to maintain "highly centralized control through decentralizing tactics" (Harvey, 1991:73). Here networking makes possible the control of others when networkers enlist and coerce new allies more rapidly than do those with whom they compete (for example, Latour 1987).

In such views of contemporary life, those who control and win out do so through exploiting these disjunctions. Indeed, the body itself becomes similarly envisioned as a site of disintegration and refabrication (Haraway 1991). A global network in the merchandizing of body parts allows quite literally for the reassembling of an individual person out of transnationally bartered bits and pieces.[22] Here again the faster one is able to mobilize networks and exploit them, the less likely that any of us will find it possible to understand what role a sense of self might play in social encounters.

Naturally, these disjunctions will always appear greatest to us when they are happening, and especially when they create instability in our own lives; for no uncertainty moves us so much than the existential one we call living. This is why institutional living promotes in the name of "seriousness" a deeply morbid version of empathy, and why, as a homeless friend of mine argues, "if you enjoy happiness, pleasure, and hedonism, you are in big trouble!"

So, what I have to offer here is not, I think, a call of the wild, but merely a call for revisiting some forms of knowledge that those with dirtier hands than yours or mine have devoted considerable empathic energies to embodying meaningfully. I say this because the disjunction we experience today cannot, at the level of having those experiences, seem anything but unsettling unless we are able to visit those events with both enthusiasm and a sense of enjoyment—with both humoral richness and with a sense of humor, if you will.

To my colleagues, therefore, who use the words "not serious" as a criticism levied in academic circles to describe those who prefer their liminal freedom to the dehumanizing tedium of institutional networking, I can only hope that at some point each of us may willfully achieve such a distinction. Clearly, once one is willing to examine the effects of social disjunction on the sense of self, it becomes easier to see why the self frets so intensely—why, that is, we are made to feel lonely in institutions of higher whatever, and concomitantly, why we seem so incapable of seeing stress as anything but harmful.

There is no reason, except for a fearing of change itself, that we should be so determined to misunderstand the often-beneficial nature of stress. Though we may recognize in the abstract that stress is the primary catalyst for creative as well as destructive transformation, we will rarely sense its positive potential where life becomes characterized by an absence of collective encounters in which the presence of another leads to some creative mutation of self. And, in the absence of such collective moments, it becomes obvious why feeling like an outsider may be our most predominantly shared sensibility. In developmental terms, then, it may as easily be the case that things in the postmodern world are actually *slowing down*, that entropy reigns when we turn a blind eye to the frisson—the excitement—of the exotic.

Considered in this light, it may actually be the case that the self, in fact, *changes less* in this condition of "amodernity" than it might have when the structural inversions characteristic of collective rites of passage encouraged us to think more positively about the outcome of stressful encounters. This conclusion is, perhaps, the most unsettling one that postmodernity begs: that in our foregoing the interpersonal merging of self and other in orchestrated moments of danger, we may now find ourselves not only wholly incapable of change, but also wholly capable of believing that we are constantly changing. Here the consequence of so neglecting the body's senses may well be that we refuse even to consider the all-too-real probability that our self-induced love of alienation is part of the morbid outcome of taking oneself far too seriously.

Chapter 3

The Writing of Passage

Those who do not get outside of themselves are all of a piece.
—*Vauvenargues*

The Politics of Inexperience

There are experiences in life that most of us will never have. Not long ago an Italian friend of mine disclosed over dinner the fact that his now elderly father was doing less well than he had hoped with a recent illness because he was the last surviving member of a large family and was finding the loneliness difficult. This he said in such a plain voice that the circumstances of his father's loneliness might easily have been set aside for another topic of conversation. However, after a pause, and I really don't know why, I asked him that idle question we so often raise when conversation flags. "How many children were in his family?" I inquired. He hesitated, looked at me apologetically, and then announced, "Twenty-four."

"Twenty-four children!" I thought. "What could such a household be like?" For a long moment I stood there stupefied and lost for words. We just stared at each other. Then, I turned away and wandered across the lawn. Now recalling the event, I am sure he watched me as we parted, looking for that aimless staggering that no doubt he had many times before induced in others by this announcement. In my mind's eye, I could see him looking at me sorrowfully, knowing quite well that I would never fully imagine the living conditions in such a home—if, that is, one could call "home" whatever kind of building or buildings this small civilization occupied.

Being one who by profession claims an interest in other modes of living, my bubble had burst; for visualizing this family presented more of a challenge than did any kind of kin relation I had encountered in the field. How did these twenty-four children plus two parents live together? How did they engage in simple activities like dining? Were there subunits within the tribe for managing what the rest of us might call normal family activities? Did one such unit go out to procure food? Were clothes cataloged to avoid squabbles over who wore what or to fit the needs of many growth cycles? Did this family have a single survival strategy, its own company, or were individuals left to make way on their own? Could anyone tell when a member wandered off or decided to avoid chores? Indeed, what friend or relative might even lay claim to knowing everyone's name!

For some time after my friend's announcement, I know I must have appeared stupefied, wallowing in this meditation. In a way, I even felt a bit hurt; for though my father's northern European family had kept to civilized dimensions, my mother's Sicilian clan was always sufficiently large so that I could pride myself on knowing what it was like to grow up in a crowd. Until that moment, I had always considered myself as having known in some embodied, visceral way an experience both unusual and rare in today's world. With this brief conversation that awareness seemed pedestrian, even trivial, by comparison.

Now, it seems, I regularly recall the epiphany of that moment, for it dramatizes for me better than anything else I have known what I call the "anthropological paradox." This is the paradox by which we say, on the one hand, that you have to be one to know one—that participation is the core practice of ethnography—and on the other, that the hardest thing to study is your own culture. Arguably, a family of twenty-six is far from representing "my" culture, but they had occupied a social space much like the one I had known through my mother's extended family. Indeed, they were even from the same social and linguistic group, the same "culture." By any American definition of ethnic identity, I had what it took to claim these people as mine, even if I could have more easily imagined a Martian nuclear family or a family of talking dogs.

But there was another reason why the thought of this family impressed me so. And that was its commonness. Were it not for its size, it had no distinction of the sort we call up in our imagination when we isolate the experiences of another individual as extraordinary. On their own, the children could easily have led lives that others would call normal. As adults outside of that home, nobody would necessarily have singled out any one of them as odd or remarkable, unless, perhaps, if offered the kind of information I had been given by my friend. As individuals, no member of that family need ever appear to us as other than ordinary. How odd, then, that we anthropologists go about looking for the nonordinary to dramatize difference. How odd that the examples that pepper our studies of social relations must appear to us as noteworthy. What is it, moreover, about the living out of an event that entitles us to consider ourselves experienced? Why, to extend this thought, do dramatic moments surface for us as key signals of what we as individuals, each can claim uniquely to know?

For anthropologists devoted to understanding the illness experiences of others, the problem of ordinary knowledge is more than abstract. Each time we try to come to terms with the bodily disturbances of another human being, we eject the ordinary because the event of becoming ill is also an exercise in distinguishing a particular experience as nonordinary. Illness, then, is (and probably more than any other kind of experience) an exercise in the nonordinary—the epitome of what we call consciousness, the crystallizing of self. And it is because of this recognizing process that examining ethnographically one's own illness experience causes us to reevaluate what we might possibly have in mind when we use the word "normal." For me, the realization came quite suddenly one afternoon in the summer of 1973.[1]

On a humid and hot Virginia day in that year, I accidentally drove a scythe into a nest of hornets while clearing a farm field. I remember the feeling well: in the few seconds it took to register the cause of the random intense heat of each sting, I had already been massively poisoned. In that desperate moment, I did what anyone would do: I ran.

Next to the nearby barn stood my friend Roy—a tough, weathered Appalachian man used to catastrophe. Roy had already lost his front teeth to the rim of an exploding truck tire, so when he laughed at my unusual antics, I stopped waving my arms and began to laugh too. Roy was someone I trusted. Only a few weeks earlier he had stood by me as I brought a shovel down hard on a charging copperhead, slicing it in half. He would do anything for a friendship, even if, as was usually the case, the outcome set him back. Roy had survived numerous accidents—a bulldozer rolling on him while working for the highway department up on the mountain, a crushed leg, kicks from angry cows—but he could always smile in the face of disaster.

The episode, so I thought, had come to an end as I went to the house, took off my clothes, and began to inspect the damage. Hives everywhere, some around stings, most not. When I came back outside, I felt weird. Roy tried to joke and then stopped. I remember his saying, "David . . . you don't look too good." I knew at that moment that something had gone wrong.

As it turned out, the countless stings had filled me with enough venom to make my entire body swell into a leathery second skin. I was beginning to experience anaphylaxis, the phenomenon by which the body destroys itself in shock. Had I been able to consider my condition abstractly, I would have described the feeling as quite literally "superficial," as if the tingling sensation were occurring to another body. I was enough disoriented to sense the words of others as coming from afar. I was dreaming, in some semiconscious state. I heard others speaking, but I wasn't there, or they weren't there. I was alone and becoming more so—like waking to the sound of one's name or falling to sleep only to awake to a quite different kind of reality. En route to the university hospital some twenty miles away, I recall the obsession of monitoring my heartbeat, as if by concentration I might make it more regular than I knew it then was.

I cannot say that I have any clear memory of how I ended up on my back being stared at by countless medical students. But the shock of anaphylaxis was not lessened by my now feeling like something of a lab rat. Yes, they were concerned as all future doctors must be, but they were also excited. The presiding physician could have as easily been in the lecture hall, for now he would show them how to take control of both me and my illness. Perhaps it was the anaphylaxis itself that sensitized me as a social animal on its back, but I harbored no illusions about the choreography; as the plot unfolded, my role was to be, in the first instance, helpless and, in the second, grateful. Not that I was not either of these; but I do recall clearly how my appearance had allowed for a very dramatic pedagogical event to unfold. I remember, for instance, the resident's announcement that this experience would be their first exposure to "the real thing." I remember his allowing the best of his underlings to poke futilely at my body in an attempt to insert an IV. I also remember his announcing that things "did not look good." But what I remember most was the private lecture I received when things did actually turn around a few hours later.

Sitting up with my legs dangling helplessly and my skin a mottled mass, I was summarily informed that my body could not recognize itself, that one of its safety mechanisms (one that functioned by limiting peripheral circulation in a moment of extreme stress) had done its job far too well. I was at war with myself. Were I stung again, there was a very good chance I would die, because the massive poisoning had enough sensitized me that my next reaction could be fatal. And, yes, I was reminded, if I did not stay calm throughout this ordeal, the anxiety itself could have irreversible consequences for the severity of my reaction.

Thus began my long saga as a patient without answers. In those days, the sensitivity tests were pretty crude, as was the therapy. Grind up whole bees and wasps, dissolve the powder in solution, and inject that into an allergic person. Watch the patient carefully for signs of an oncoming reaction. Increase the doses over many months until a certain tolerance seemed to be achieved. Keep the injections at that level forever. Of course, nobody really knew how a body—especially a frightened one—would respond to a real episode. A raised heartbeat, dehydration, even simple exhaustion could have a decisive influence on one's very survival.

So, knowing that my allergy was being treated clinically offered little reassurance every time I heard the buzzing of a bee—one caught indoors, blown in an open car window, or buzzing over one's lunch. Would today be the day you accidentally bumped a nest with the lawn mower, or stepped into the shoes you had left outside only to feel that feeling? Life in rural Vermont was like living in a snake pit. Actually, it was a good bit worse because even vipers do not go out of their way to seek shelter inside the very cup from which one drinks. This was a disorder ready-made for paranoia. Worse still, I was not, as a recent philosophy graduate, at all comforted by the naive ways in which my physical condition was rendered metaphysically by my clinicians. And as a new recruit to the discipline of anthropology, I wondered often about what it might mean to be thousands of miles from the sort of treatment my doctors claimed

I would require were I stung even once; for what I had been told left me with little confidence: It is not inevitable that your next sting will harm you, but you may well die. However, at all costs remain calm, because anxiety will only worsen your reaction.

Without dwelling on details, it was fairly clear to me that choosing anthropology was at least a life-threatening, if not a deadly, decision. It is easy to visualize, though: there I am walking down a dirt track in rural Southeast Asia and a wasp in flight bounces off the back of my neck, slipping into my shirt. Or maybe I have just ventured into an ancient Indian temple only to find a massive nest of swarming bees directly above my head. "Is this the moment at which my life comes to an end, or is it nothing?" I so often thought. It is an experience I have had so many times that the very idea of dying has become commonplace in my life.

Thus, the everyday world around me became a place of real threat—no enemy soldiers hiding in the brush. Does not the criminal fear the police dog more than he fears the policeman? After all, even your enemy in battle might spare you, as you might him, in a moment of human compassion. And the naïveté of my doctors about the therapy I would have to find in some of the world's poorest countries did not ease my anxieties about surviving the sort of simple sting that most everyone else takes as one of life's more minor events. Yes, there must be good hospitals where you are going, I was told. Isn't the rest of the world just like us, or at least dying to be so?

These emotions are ones that cannot be known in the abstract. So, rather than trying further to evoke them narratively, I would like to return to the diagnostic moment when the hospital resident labeled me "the real thing" for his clinical neophytes, because at that moment my destiny was enough dependent on his actions that my desire to survive far overshadowed my awareness that he was using—even appropriating—my suffering as a part of what made his life worthwhile. In owing my life to modern medicine, there was little need for that doctor or his students to tread gently on my knowledge of what I owed them. Indeed, within minutes my marginal experience became the center of what they lived to control; even my fear was fuel for their confidence. For them, the unnamed was named—the bizarre made "classical."

My transformation into a state of well-being then was exchanged for their tranformation into accomplished clinicians. My revivification, a part of their heroization. The exchange was for me more than fair (after all, I did come away alive); but the nature of our respective transformations—and this is my point—was extraordinarily different: for me, a catalyst for years of uncertainty; for them, a reward for having been loyal achievers. While my uncertainty lived on for years, they had gotten from this encounter the certainty they needed.

"Don't ever let yourself be taken to a teaching hospital," a leading AIDS researcher once recommended over dinner. Today it has become fashionable for medical anthropologists to recount precisely the sorts of anxieties about clinical encounters that I have herein summarized. But what makes the medical anthropologist different from the clinician? Are not anthropologists equally engaged in an act of appropriating the experiences of others? And if they are, what sort of transformation does such appropriation facilitate for them?

Driver's-Side Airbag

In a commentary about truth and disbelief, Mark Twain noted that the first duty of every human being is "to think about himself until he has exhausted the subject, then he is in a condition to take up minor interests and think of other people." Twain's sarcasm about our occasionally indulging ourselves in another's well-being was, of course, directed toward what he thought to be the crude self-interest that characterizes life in general; but it might as well have been a metaphysical judgment of the reflexive entrapments of the post-Enlightenment world, in which one falls repeatedly toward oneself in the mirror of self-concern, toward an endless process of validating the authenticity of one's experiences by appropriating the "sensational" moments, the extreme experiences, of others.

In fact, while medical anthropologists question the objectives of medical practitioners—whose treatment of patients as "cases" robs sufferers of their identities—anthropologists are themselves often never so deeply entranced than by the prospect of convincing their readers that they are personally experienced in the ways of suffering. We do this primarily by laying claim—often by just staking that claim—to some deeper meaning. While doctors may be content with "curing"—with simply altering the course of something pathological that they may not profess to understand completely—the authority of medical anthropology rests more often than not upon whether one can speak convincingly about another's suffering. This is why we so often claim to be "giving voice" to those whom we represent—why we promote ethnographic conventions that unite our private perceptions with a narrative control over that which we witness.

Because of the degree and kind of control that the "giving of voice" can require, Nichols (1981) quite provocatively, as mentioned in the Preface, compares ethnography with pornography; for both are highly inauthentic in their structuring of affect, both are manipulative of what we are allowed to acknowledge as psychologically relevant, and both are dependent upon a kind of expository realism in which we place ourselves between the distanced observer and the subject observed. This is also why, in this line of arguing, it is so common for medical anthropologists to "stand up" for the voices they claim to represent—to be openly sympathetic and emotional about their informants—even while sometimes denigrating the subjective claims of their fellow anthropologists who write and speak of their own suffering.

Setting aside the undignified squabbling over experience that is endemic to my field, it is clear that ethnographers are often at their most insecure when upstaged by another's experience in the trenches. Confronted with an experiential domain beyond their own knowing, they are left with but two alternatives: remain silent in the face of the extraordinary—which, by the way, is also why those engaged in true life-and-death clinical struggles so rarely write about them, or assimilate what they observe of the experiences of others as aspects of their own heroic quest—to haul their ethnographic prey into a setting such as this very document I am now writing, and place another's fear and true liminality on the altar of one's own moral indignation.

The problems here are multiple. In the first case—that of silent suffering— the ill become exceedingly vulnerable to other's fantasies, both because they may be disinclined to give up the sacred dimensions of their private liminality, but also because their silence makes possible an "open season" for those who make a business of such appropriating. And with the odds so heavily in favor of authors who appropriate, is it any wonder that the "writing of passage" has become an industry plagued with that kind of greatness which borders on tyranny?

Like the patient at the mercy of an arrogant physician (and whom among us hasn't met one?), those struggling with illness find themselves especially vulnerable to writers who may be caught up in their own private search for authority. These authors remain totally free to fantasize about the power of representation, because the silent sufferer may have long since exited the arena of petty social discourse. As Halpern argues in his study of Biblical megalomania, this habit of literature is one wherein we "seem forever to be talking about the "marginalized," and the "oppressed," and pretending to represent them. But there is nothing marginal about those with the power to express their views, for they at least have the opportunity to persuade others. The truly marginal are those who are not even suffered to speak. And the most marginal of all are those who have passed, silent, from history" (2001:xv). It is perhaps this final fear of anonymity that more than any other fear provides the catalyst for writing; for it takes little imagination to grasp how illness authors especially resemble those paranoid tyrants of old who, as Canetti beautifully argued (1960), could not imagine anything so horrific as their own premature demise. Indeed, because of the subtle shift from a genuine experience of pain to the authorial appropriation of another's suffering, the literature on illness experience becomes especially vulnerable to vicarious self-promotion. This shift is what Stoller intends to redress when he—perhaps more graciously—recommends that scholars adopt the "respectfully decentered conception and practice of depicting social life" (1997:26) that characterizes the outlook of West African storytellers, who "are humbled by history, which consumes the bodies of those who attempt to talk it, write it, or film it."

Thus, while the reasons that might cause one to corral the somatic experiences of another are many, three dimensions of writing about illness make medical anthropology particularly vulnerable to this temptation to appropriate:

1) a fear of going it alone—that is, a tendency to cling to institutional settings when confronted with the pain and uncertainty of human suffering;
2) a deep ambivalence about change—that is, a reticence about taking the risks that are the necessary precondition for human transformation, and the consequent tendency to project one's ambivalence by vicariously experiencing the illness of someone else; and
3) a discomfort with one's own mortality—that is, the need to lionize one's involvement in another's suffering as a way of accruing interest on one's own moral investment.

In consort, these three dimensions of my field are what can lead to the airbag's placement on the driver's side alone, to the airbag's strategic deployment when the words it contains are needed to avoid taking risks, and to the heroic narrative that can unfold with impunity once one's ethnographic passenger gets launched through the windshield. Here the question is not what a driver's-side airbag is but who may have the dubious distinction of being called one.

Inscribing Experience as an Academic Industry

While it has become customary for medical anthropologists to scoff at the tribal allegiance of careerist doctors and bench scientists to the institutions that depersonalize those who suffer, let us not forget that we too are equally culpable; for it is not only scientists who, as Latour writes, "speak in the name of new allies that they have shaped and enrolled [in order to] tip the balance of force in their favor" (1987:259). Indeed, we "gain nothing in explaining 'natural' sciences by invoking 'social' sciences. In fact, there is not the slightest difference," he argues, "between the two, and they are both to be studied in the same way." Thus, the social sciences may require even more skepticism, because they profess to be analyzing the very networks that they so busily are building (256).[2]

What is clear for economics, politics and management is all the clearer for sociology itself. How could someone who decided to follow scientists in action forget to study sociologists striving to define what society is all about, what keeps us all glued together, how many classes there are, what is the aim of living in society, what are the major trends in its evolution? . . . The very definition of 'society' is the final outcome, in Sociology Departments, in Statistical Institutions, in journals, of other scientists busy at work gathering surveys, questionnaires, archives, records of all sorts, arguing together, publishing papers, organizing other meetings. Any agreed definition marks the happy end of controversies. . . . No more, no less. The results on what society is made of do not spread more or faster than those of economics, topology or particle physics. These results too would die if they went outside of the tiny networks so necessary for their survival. . . .

A sociologist's interpretation of society will not be substituted for what every one of us thinks of society without additional struggle, without textbooks, chairs in universities, positions in government, integration in the military, and so on, exactly as for geology, meteorology or statistics." (256–57)

So, sociologists (and anthropologists) are just as dependent upon their networks of power as are members of the fields they come to study. However, our vulnerability to not seeing this situation is, if anything, increased because as analysts it is that much harder for us to accept that our authority is subject to the same forms of professional consent as is the authority of those we study. As Lovelock has written,

You may think of the academic scientist as the analogue of the independent artist. In fact, nearly all scientists [anthropologists being no exception] are employed by some large organization, such as a governmental department, a university, or a multinational company. . . . They may think that they are free, but in reality they are, nearly all of them, employees; they have traded freedom of thought for good working conditions, a steady income, tenure, and a pension. They are also constrained by an army of bureaucratic forces, from the funding agencies to the health and safety organizations. . . . To cap it all, in recent years the "purity" of science is ever more closely guarded by a self-imposed inquisition called the peer review. This well-meaning but narrow-minded nanny of an institution ensures that scientists work according to conventional wisdom and not as curiosity or inspiration moves them. Lacking freedom they are in danger of succumbing to a finicky gentility or of becoming, like medieval theologians, the creatures of dogma. (1990:19)

This unacknowledged dependence on institutions and institutional networks is precisely why we have become so embroiled in the notion of rhetorical entitlement—that is, with what one individual can or cannot be allowed to say. For here, more than anywhere, we are easily embarrassed by the degree to which we have merely fought to replace one system of knowledge—one episteme—with another that may be equally draconian. This entitlement is often most rigorously protected when we feel that our turf is being set upon by upstarts, even while we may actually share that turf with what we think to be the seemingly harmless outsider.

In a wonderful commentary on British society, for example, the Canadian novelist Margaret Atwood once described how this code of silencing—of protecting a domain of rhetorical entitlement—actually works. Referring to the English class system as a "sixth sense," Atwood remarks of those who police culture that they

are covered with prickles, like sea urchins, and these are activated by speech. Open your mouth and you're placed, and treated accordingly. Class isn't just poor people versus rich people. Each class, each subclass of each class, has its loyalties and traditions, and a bit of contempt for those of the others. As a foreigner, however, you have a big advantage: you're classless. Your voice, for them, is white sound: it has no resonance, awakens no memories, provokes no knee-jerk responses. So you can talk to anyone, and you'll often be answered with less caution and more warmth than if you were English. (1988:2)

Though I am not too sure about the "white noise" of most Americans, Atwood's remarks about the British serve very well in sensitizing us to how fieldworkers who specialize in the emotional pageantry of others' lives can succeed through emotional distance, despite what their claims may be to the contrary. Being emotionally "near"—that is, emotionally influenced—by another may, in fact, be a distinct disadvantage for participant-observers, especially if their real goal is to transcend the policing of empathy.

In like manner, it is also the case that our liberal academics can become quite successful at seizing society's center stage, because the liberal's allegiance to dominant systems of power may be less overt than, say, the allegiances of those whose loyalties to the status quo are openly acknowledged. Just because, for instance, we have in the United States dozens of conservative think tanks for every liberal or progressive one, those liberals or progressives are not any less subject to or free from the structural mechanisms of the political life with which they are engaged. Indeed, they may be equally or more dependent because that dependence remains covert.

Though one's anthropological diploma is undoubtedly itself a kind of entitlement, we far too easily assume that our education provides us with some form of moral guarantee—as if our laziness, or fear about questioning that entitlement, is justified by the canonical symbols (diplomas, fellowships, named chairs) that can be marshaled forward to shelter us from experience. We are, thus, never so excited than by the prospect of some badge of merit that would pave the way for less and less emotion work—never so vexed or fatigued than by the prospect of having to negotiate with genuine difference. These are conditions of professional life, moreover, that are in no way alleviated in anthropology by the habits of coauthorship, where multiauthored publications become statements of allegiance, professional coats of arms. In fact, in humanistic anthropology, where real personal tragedy is daily fare, the problem is, if anything, more acute.

At the risk of being overly critical, one must confront the evidence, evidence that is easily seen in our academic obsession with research scale, with global issues, and with bombastic claims about something that, if nothing else, is *very big*—in fact, so big that its size can all but eliminate the now-mundane moral need to be human. It is not, in other words, just a war of turf—a contest within our academic herd for a piece of rhetorical terrain—but a focusing on scale as a way of appearing too important to be confused ever again with things less than superior. In the end, our all-too-real subjects—if, that is, we have ever to actually bother with them to begin with—become ready evidence for world-altering strategies that leave us looking, for lack of another descriptor, Napoleonic.

That which replaces a network of social entitlement can quickly become as uncurious about difference as what it replaces. Our liberal academics become as reactionary as their rivals because they never genuinely question their own dogmas. This lack of curiosity about those working outside of our individual networks is then not something that can be placed solely on the shoulders of the uneducated. Quite the contrary; lethargy thrives precisely in the places where its existence is rigorously denied. And, in the end, what is lost is any possibility for redefining the boundaries of what is relevant—the humor, tragedy, irony, and fragile subtlety—all of the curious traits, in other words, that are eroded by the self-righteous appropriation of another's experience.

Such a limited sense of curiosity is, then, much more insidious than it may at first appear; for any engagement with difference can only be transformative if the terms of transformation—the vocabularies of change—are negotiated through some form of mutuality. By this I mean experiential events in which some interactive risk or chance—some giving up of one's authority—becomes the catalyst for a kind of creativity that is new, redefining, and much greater than any individual achievement. Here it is easy to be more concrete. One need only look at the worldwide evidence for rites of passage, in which individuals are depersonalized and merge, to see how destructive are the values that we apply to the process of "giving voice," and the role of that process in propping up our standards of professional success.

So, let's cut the rhetorical cant in anthropology about our relative abilities to exist outside of the social networks we study and accept openly our allegiance to those same institutions. Let's at least have the decency, in other words, to admit that it is not just the wealthy lawyers, surgeons, and policymakers who just love being at Oxford, Harvard, and Stanford. And while acknowledging this true love of ours, let's also examine what happens when the desperate marginality of those who are seriously ill gets fed up to all of us in the safety of such settings.

After all, the importance of consciously making such a confession cannot be underestimated; for despite having retained some intuitive understanding that transformation and growth are important, at times we have so lost any real curiosity for the unknown that we actually believe that replacing one standard with another will, in fact, free us from the rhetoric of failure that constitutes the other real—if unacceptable—alternative. This is why those whose institutional allegiances run deepest can only think philanthropically after they have assured themselves that they cannot be intellectually dethroned.

This is also why our (especially literary) theorists go on about "revising the canon"—why, that is, academics focus so much attention on replacing one set of standards with other, no less rigid ones—without realizing that it is the reciprocity between the canonical and the acanonical that is really important. And just what canon is at stake? The answer most certainly can now be isolated by a revised assessment of what happens when one writes about another's suffering.

Anthropology as Munchausen's-by-proxy

In 1958, the anthropologist William Caudill published *The Psychiatric Hospital as a Small Society*. The book was telling not only because it marks a very early example of the study of illness as a social construction, but also because Caudill entered a psychiatric hospital, his field of research, by fabricating his own illness. In this regard, his becoming a patient was not at all unlike the behavior made famous by Baron von Munchausen, that most legendary of hypochondriacs. Like von Munchausen, Caudill's psychiatric disorder was feigned so as to experience it clinically, socially, and personally. While von Munchausen's need to become a participant-observer appears to us as a kind of pathology, at some level it is not at all unlike what for Caudill became his fieldwork.

Indeed, like the sufferer of Munchausen's syndrome, the anthropologist also accepts the notion that self-conscious imitation—even feigned participation—is how one gets close to "the real thing." Doing and observing what one's subject does—we call it participant-observation—is the most common form of fieldwork. Yes, it is true that Caudill's work would not pass the close scrutiny of a contemporary human subjects committee, but by degrees, every anthropologist who consciously decides to become a participant-observer is engaging in an act of imitation. In fact, Lévy-Bruhl (1949) actually focused on the function of imitating in what has been widely accepted as the classic meditation on anthropological participation. So how far off is the comparison?

Surely, to such an analogy, the fieldworker would respond with the charge that the anthropologist differs from sufferers of the psychiatric disorder by virtue of the ends which his means justify. For the anthropologist, the search for truth makes his projections moral, while for the individual with Munchausen's syndrome, the agonistic clinical experience becomes its own disingenuous end, where the intrigue of feigning illness overshadows any concern about the long-term consequences for those who are drawn into the ruse.

Yet, increasingly, anthropologists are aware of their inability to control the effects of participant-observation, especially when they also identify themselves as advocates for those whom they study. Festinger's now famous theory of cognitive dissonance was argued on the backs of members of a religious sect who came to believe that he and fellow researchers were emissaries, admitted into households on the grounds that they were spacemen (Festinger et al. 1964:234–38). And in studies of religion, where strong beliefs provide powerful emic interpretations of a researcher's presence, even the most overt methods will sometimes fail to limit the local effects of a researcher's intervention. In case after case, the appearance of a researcher who names herself as such causes not only the reaffirmation of religious beliefs, but also their zealous proliferation.

Students who go out to interview religious fundamentalists for anthropological research papers are, I have found, always alarmed to discover that despite their careful explaining of the reasons for the field visit, their subjects remain convinced that their arrival is the work of God herself. This is, to be clear, not a simple form of cognitive dissonance—a kind of phenomenal misunderstanding—but an example of the all-too-neglected manner in which bringing something to consciousness reifies behavior in one's subject. The projection of one's own agenda, in other words, has the quantum effect of inducing a conscious redefining by a subject of his ontological placement—a placement that, in turn, we observe and record.

And there is a Munchausen's version of this kind of projection that looks all too frighteningly like the darker side of fieldwork. Psychiatrists refer to this clinical syndrome as Munchausen's-by-proxy. Here, it is not one's own symptoms that are feigned, but those of the empathic family member or concerned friend of an illness victim. In Munchausen's-by-proxy, an illness is induced in another so as to make possible a treatment scenario in which one is not the patient, but the feigned advocate of the sufferer. How structurally different, we may ask, is the process of conducting fieldwork? Well, not very. Indeed, time after time, our work as anthropologists looks more like Munchausen's-by-proxy—in which our fieldwork itself becomes the catalyst for a redefining of indigenous identities—and less like Munchausen's original syndrome, which invites us to feign, as participant-observers, another's world view.

So, the first problem with participant-observation in anthropology is that the subject and object can merge, but in ways that are understood quite differently by each party. Though the problem applies to all sorts of ethnographic work, it is especially prevalent when an anthropologist becomes an open advocate for those with whom he or she works—when ethnographers openly valorize their subjects—and/or, paradoxically, when one is dealing with distinctly different modes of thinking. Especially where diverse cosmologies or religious beliefs are involved, we see time and again how participant-observation is not only a feigning activity, but one that can make the ethnographer the catalyst and controller of new, sometimes surprisingly unexpected, indigenous encounters. Stoller (1989), for instance, finds that the death of his sorcerer-mentor leads to familial anger and jealousy over privileged information the deceased is believed to have imparted to the ethnographer, and in a popular account of his travels through Bali, Abram (1984–85) finds that his magical tricks are no entertainment for local healers who take up the magician's challenge and almost take his life to boot!

Even when ethnographers are fortunate enough to have a good sense of how they will be redefined by their research subjects, they frequently find themselves with an indigenous identity they would rather forget. Danforth, in his remarkable ethnography of Greek firewalking and religious healing, finds that he has been labeled a categorical woman. And those studying mental illness in China find that getting inside Chinese society is made easier than usual because, like anthropologists, the insane are understood as "the outsider within." Here outsiders—that is, anthropologists—and lunatics are placed at the same remove from close blood relatives—that is, at the farther reaches of concentric domains of meaning. Chinese mental illness is then an absolutely perfect domain of anthropological research because the anthropologist is—like the mentally insane—by definition like the indigenous *outsider*.

In all of these instances, the ethnographic experience has an eerie similarity to Munchausen's-by-proxy; for when do we know except in hindsight that our attempts to achieve something like an indigenous awareness—even when carried out with compassion and true sympathy—did not have disastrous pathological outcomes for those encountered in fieldwork? Like the famous Balinese "magic by wrong address," in which magical spells ricochet and strike unwary people nearby (Wikan 1990), the anthropologist-gone-native can often displace local powers in unexpected and highly unpredictable ways and be transformed or not transformed by a willingness to get outside of the self. The problem is, if anything, exacerbated when dealing with another's illness, because that illness invariably invites some heightened self-awareness on the part of the person who must embody it.

The Writing of Passage

"Let's face it: everyone likes a story," a literary agent and friend once told me. "If you want your work to be broadly read, then make sure you tell lots of good stories. People want to hear stories. The theories are far too abstract." For most of us this dictum seems reasonable enough. Stories provide a place for imaginative projection, a space where one can see oneself as another, a domain in which specific behaviors can be understood as a function of events that are dynamically related. Moreover, by extension, those who write stories succeed in that enterprise by allowing themselves to project imaginatively into the narratives they invent, to see themselves as their characters. At times, writers are so successful at this that their readers will not accept that what they write is other than the true version of events they have actually lived. Joseph Conrad was never so taken than by the fact that criminals and law-enforcement officials reading *The Secret Agent* (1907) actually were convinced that he must have been engaged in the very activities about which he wrote. Likewise, the longstanding debate about the veracity of Carlos Castaneda's *The Teachings of Don Juan* (1968) was fueled not only by the author's position as an anthropology graduate student, but also by his accurate and intimate knowledge of the psychoactive drugs around which his story unfolds.

Permit me, then, by way of concluding, to outline four areas of general concern in representing the bodily transformations of others.

PROBLEM 1: THE VIEW FROM AFAR

In fiction, fusing with one's characters has always been a process of becoming another person. As Gide provocatively states: "I have no interest in my own opinion. I am no longer someone, but several. . . . Push abnegation," he advises, "to the point of complete self-oblivion" (1926 [in Buckler 1961:241]).

But while novelists fuse with characters, medical anthropologists attempt to fuse with real people who are in a physical state that we cannot directly know without having had the same affliction. Writing about illness is in this sense an entirely different enterprise—despite what postmodernists may argue—than is novel writing. In medical anthropology, we have no proscriptions against a perfectly healthy individual's elaboration of another's tragedy, though as "givers of voice" such proscriptions ought to be considered fully. I remember, for instance, speaking with a famous Navajo healer about her not having treated a difficult pregnancy. She was astonished that I should even have considered her as an appropriate healer; for unlike her aunt who provided the service, she had not herself had that illness.

You cannot profess to know another's suffering any more than you can cure what you have not had. You cannot communicate with an alienated sufferer—as any student of Jungian psychology knows well—unless you can fully see yourself as engaging, under other circumstances, in the same pathology. Those who attempt the task are feigning that illness—that is, projecting an anthropological form of Munchausen's-by-proxy—for they will always be gathering information from inaccessible fields by assuming some unearned intimacy.

PROBLEM 2: NARRATING THE UNSPEAKABLE

Health-care activists frequently discover that their well-intentioned efforts to explore another's illness fall flat or, worse yet, deeply offend those sufferers. I know hospice volunteers who become outright angry because a dying individual for whom they were meant to be caring refused to acknowledge openly—and in the presence of the "caregiver"—his or her own mortality. Medical anthropologists assume that an understanding of another's suffering must consist of an explication of the emotional details of another's illness, even though we all know that the liminality of suffering may create spaces that are rightly inaccessible, even sacred. Here I can think of two personal friends (one with cancer, another with AIDS) who had no interest in sharing their pain publicly or even in exploring that pain privately. Though I was very close to both of them, the friend with AIDS said it all in one sentence: "David, some day we'll have to talk"—which, of course, in deference to his integrity, we never did nor should ever have.

The crime of displaying in full view these unspeakable dimensions of illness rests squarely on the shoulders of medical anthropology, for we, more than others, must be aware of rules against speaking, especially where indigenous beliefs prohibit it. The Balinese, for instance, are quite fearful that their own words will invoke the very hazards they hope to transcend. Moreover, their fears are not exceptional; the phenomenon is frequently recorded, even among indigenous groups resettled in cosmopolitan contexts—as, for example, in Fadiman's description of such proscriptions among Hmong refugees in central California (1997). Here the problem is not only one of speaking the unspeakable, but also of creating a narrative to represent the emotional life of individuals who may have no understanding of, nor use for, it.

Without quibbling about who can claim "to know," one need only examine a more harmless example of this disjunction in popular anthropological writing. When Marjorie Shostak decided that to be a successful fieldworker she "needed the !Kung to start speaking for themselves" (1983:7), she sought out individuals who were known for their storytelling abilities. An exchange with an "able storyteller" who told Shostak she was wasting her time with other women says it all. The voice is Shostak's:

"Bey, we've already talked about how people still remember some of their childhood experiences, no matter how old they are. You agreed and said that was true for yourself. Won't you tell me about things you still remember?"

"Yes, I certainly remember things from my childhood. I am old and have experienced much. You ask me about something and I'll tell you about it."

"Why don't you tell me about anything that comes into your mind about your childhood, something that has stayed with you over the years."

"Are you saying that people don't remember their childhoods? They do. Ask me and I'll tell you."

"Tell me about the things your mother and father did."

"Fine. They brought me up, gave me food, and I grew and grew and then I was an adult. That's what they did."

"Do you remember any specific time, maybe when they did something wonderful or perhaps, something you didn't like?"

"You are asking me well. Parents sometimes help children and sometimes scold them."

"Did your parents ever scold you?"

"Are you saying that a parent doesn't scold a child? Children do senseless things and their parents scold them."

"What did you do that was senseless?"

"I ruined things, just like my granddaughter. Why this very morning she ruined some things in the hut and my daughter-in-law hit her. Do you think a parent doesn't scold a child? No, a parent scolds a child, then the child learns sense."

"Bey, we are talking very well together; I know you are old and have experienced many things . . ."

"Many things, ehey, mother . . ."

". . . but I want to talk only about you, not about anyone else. I want to know about things you experienced, things your mother did when you were small, and what you did as you grew up, married, and had children. So far we have been talking about things in a general way, in a way that everyone would agree with. That's good. But now, let's talk more specifically about things that happened to you, about any time in your life."

"Yes, we are talking very well. You keep asking me and I'll keep telling you. I am old and know many things."

"I am asking you. But I cannot tell you what memories to speak about. Only you know what you've experienced. Try to tell me something about something your parents or your siblings did; or what happened when you menstruated, when you married, or had children; or, about your family, your co-wife, your husband, . . . anything you'd like. Only it has to be about you."

"Yes . . . we have already talked about my mother and my father and how I ruined things. Now ask me about other things and I will tell you. I am old and know. Those other women are children and still haven't taught themselves. I have seen a lot. I really know. You ask me and I'll tell you."(37)

The same disinterest in florid narrative is parodied in a well-known skit by hippie comedians Cheech and Chong. Asked to write a grade-school essay about the previous summer's vacation, each student's story begins with the same mantra: "On the first day of my summer vacation, I got up. . . ." For whom, we might legitimately ask, are the impassioned narratives of medical anthropology actually written? Is it possible that nobody wants to hear Bey's narrative because there is no stylized pathos to render affectively? Numerous other such fieldwork examples exist that one might cite, but the disjunction in narrative expectations is obvious.

PROBLEM 3: THE "FRISSON" OF THE UNLAWFUL

Clinical writing is like travel writing in that both explore things that are not, in general, familiar. What else, we may ask, do these two apparently quite different genres share?

In a collection of essays on travel, the literary critic Paul Fussell (1987) states that a traveler is subjected—as Lord Byron once said of this activity as well as, tellingly, of gambling and battle—to an intense emotional agitation that is inseparable from the accomplishment itself. That the word "travel", invokes *travail*—that is, strenuous toil, hardship, even anguish and agony—Fussell says, reminds us of the homesickness, the loneliness, and the fear that accompanies the pensive wonder of experiencing the strange. Here, indeed, the illness and the journey are one and the same.

Fussell then might as well have been speaking about illness, for the sensitive traveler, he goes on, "will also feel a degree of guilt at his alienation from ordinary people . . . [and] if a little shame doesn't mingle with the traveler's pleasure, there is probably going to be insufficient ironic resonance in his perceptions" (1987:15). Short of assenting to Strabo's ancient conviction that travelers had to be liars—"for if a traveler doesn't visit his narrative with the spirit and techniques of fiction, no one will want to hear it" (16)—Fussell concludes the introduction to his compendium by arguing that good travel writing must juggle two poles by making a reader aware of a lot of *things* while demonstrating in the opposite direction that these otherwise inert objects or phenomena are elements of a much larger metaphysical—and, ultimately, ethical—meaning. Illness writing is, in each of these respects, no different.

But while good travel writing stands or falls on its ability to merge the accomplishment with the agitation of the risky experiences of which Byron spoke, good illness ethnography must suppress its emotional excitation, or when it shows it, present it as its subject's embodied experience. Thus, despite the intention of postmodern anthropology to involve ethnographers in a new and active description of "otherness," anthropologists—contemporary or traditional—are united in their open exploration of another's travails. Indeed, the only thing that holds their experiences together as "anthropological" is the claim that they are ethnographic—that is, that they partake of a certain experiential validity that is legitimized by not being oneself trapped within another's workaday world, but, at the same time, being able to represent that world. The traveler can readily leave the habitat of the foreign land he visits in the same way that the medical anthropologist need bear no daily responsibility for those whose stories he exacts.

Behind every medical ethnographer is, we must then presume, an emotionally committed individual whose ethical behavior entitles him or her to excise the "frisson of the unlawful," to escape "from the traveler's domestic identity" into a world of strangers where "a new sense of selfhood can be tried on, like a costume" (13). It is for this reason that so-called reflexive anthropology is, in the end, a depressingly reactionary endeavor (Spencer 1989): the effect of bringing subjectivity to the front of one's discussion is not only that one properly eschews the general for that which is "experience-near," but also that one ends up adopting "a literary practice which tries above all to close the hermeneutic circle by limiting [one's] readers' access to that which [one] wants to interpret for [oneself]" (149).

Though these overtly "reactionary" aspects of postmodernism have been repeatedly considered, they will always create ill-ease when they are presented in accounts of the travails of others; for the question of "confidence" must necessarily loom large whenever postmodernism is taken seriously (Lemert 1997). Now suppressing one's own emotional excitation while presenting it as another's embodied experience is a fairly good definition not only of fieldwork, but also (as we have just seen) of some of our most peculiar clinical disorders. What matters here is less the postmodern lament that an anthropologist—in suppressing his or her own "reflexes"—may resemble rather more the confidence man than the tourist or journalist, but that anthropologists necessarily embody the post-Enlightenment need to experience vicariously both another's transformation and one's own authority in roughly equal doses.

What this means is, first, that anthropological writings—including the explication of the illness narratives of others—implicitly contain elements common to all rites of passage. For it is in rites of passage alone that a new personality may be experienced not as a costume, but—to paraphrase

Fussell—as an intense emotional activity inseparable from the accomplishment itself. "All the pathos and irony of leaving one's youth behind is—implicit in every joyous moment of travel: one knows that the first joy can never be recovered, and the wise traveler learns not to repeat successes but tries new places all the time" (Fussell 1987:14). As with travel, so too must we illness narrators accept the fact that we are often moved toward the theoretically ridiculous by our fear of being moved, against our wills, by the socially mundane. Our passion for the way things are done elsewhere, that is, is frequently mitigated by a private desire not to be confused with the person next door.

These are a few reasons why so many illness narratives end up looking more like covert hero epics about their authors. But there are other reasons too.

PROBLEM 4: THE SELF-MADE HERO

By now it ought to be fairly clear that one of the central arguments of this chapter is that in writing narratives of illnesses we have not experienced, we inadvertently become sightseers, tourists of another's tragedy, unless, that is, we can convince our readers that our presence is mandated by the salvation needs of those about whom we write. If not for the implicit or explicit demonstration of the medical anthropologist's valor, he would surely feel as external to the illness experiences he witnesses as any tourist who observes a new and novel event. This is why the illness narrative genre is plagued by the not-so-subtle heroizing of we authors who give voice (and hence life) to those we represent.

Must all illness ethnographies written about inaccessible domains be heroic? Probably; for what reader has the intellectual interest or the patience to learn about the ethnographer's failures—to congratulate Loring Danforth (1989), for instance, for crying openly because he cannot experience the religious healing of Greek firewalkers. Thus by proving that the salvation needs of those for whom we give voice justifies our speaking for them, we inadvertently fall prey to the heroic narratives that legitimize our presence in that foreign place—one so accurately labeled by DiGiacomo as a "kingdom of the sick" (1987).

Indeed, our cultural responses to illness confirm this assessment in other crucial settings. Medical students must prove that they can enter this kingdom and exit it unscathed if they are to earn the respect of their mentors and professional peers. Doctors are trained not to become psychologically sick by the emotional contagion of their patients' suffering. And when they actually do write about learning to achieve that distance—that is, when they write about medical school—they time and again use that same heroic voice to demonstrate to their readers that they are survivors of this inhumane system—even if, as Pollock (1996) has cleverly shown, their "outsider's" stance is almost universally shared by their fellow students.

Here the heroic medical student is, in fact, reiterating less the dehumanizing nature of medical education than the loss of autonomy that threatens to remove the medical practitioner from the bright lights of her own private epic. As Pollock points out, these training tales "adopt a seductively radical mask for the promotion of fundamentally conservative values in the play of medical power" (354). Indeed, those who write them appear largely "opaque to the possibility that the institutions of medical education and training might in some sense be organized precisely to create this process of experiences, feelings, and beliefs" (350). "It is not surprising [then] that training tales may be read as discourses on power; what is remarkable is the misdirection achieved by physician-authors when their nostalgia for power is transformed into a discourse on 'care' and compassion" (355). What, one may reasonably ask, exonerates medical anthropology from the same charge?

A hero cannot fulfill his destiny without having the power in place to transcend successfully the various trials that are part of the educational process of becoming a doctor. Indeed, while medical schools can marshal forward impressive statistics that illustrate their levels of hyperdiversity—their variability, that is, by indicators such as race, ethnicity, national origin, age, marital status, or gender preference—they remain almost completely homogenous when one controls for the desire of those same students to occupy a chair directly beneath the bright lights that illuminate the heroic dimensions of the field. In fact, one can draw a direct correlation between the ratings of the so-called "best" medical schools and their level of homogeneity in this regard. Students at, say, Johns Hopkins, or Harvard, or Stanford typically no more want to work in domains where their professional skills are not applauded than are the medical-school professors who teach them interested in teaching at the kind of small college that I do.

Recording others' illness narratives then becomes not only a way of giving voice to illness sufferers, but also a mechanism by which those who write experience for themselves the health benefits of disclosing the story they want to tell. In having this need, anthropologists are no different than anyone else. As Pennebaker has admirably demonstrated, the very process of encoding our travails in narrative has the effect of healing our anxieties and discomforts about being in a strange, anxiety-generating space (2001). Uncomfortable places, in fact, everywhere provoke the need for whatever powers may be necessary to transcend them—whether such places involve another's clinical tragedy, or some domain of medicine in which practitioners must forego the praise of their professional skills by teachers and colleagues. It is not then the patient who is healed by the narrative projections of illness writing, but the writer himself whose outlook improves markedly by the placement of his emotional uncertainty into words.

Chapter 4

Running in Place

> *"What if a biography were to tell about* desire, *not achievement . . . ?*
> —*bell hooks,* Outlaw Culture: Resisting Representations

The Catalytic Converter

For the past several years I have run a nonprofit, the purpose of which is to make possible mentoring opportunities for undergraduates in areas not easily served by traditional liberal arts colleges.[1] Though I had been arranging such opportunities for nearly two decades, some health-care research I conducted for my state medical society in the early 1990s[2] had enabled me to meet a special group of physicians who, once identified, turned out to be excellent teachers and loyal mentors to my students. What made this group of physicians so unusual—as well as so helpful—was their independence and a concomitant willingness to thrive in remote areas. These were individuals whose conditions of work necessitated some ability to survive without the accolades that are regularly poured upon their professional peers who cannot exist outside of the academic networks that regularly reward them. These people were, in other words, individuals who could survive happily without the constant need for what the British call "the bright lights."

Among the many things that this group of physicians shared was the value they universally placed upon health-related experiences occurring early in life. Though these experiences varied enormously—volunteer work, a family illness, a traumatic event—they unanimously attributed their ability to survive and be happy enough to work independently to some early, sensitizing, emotional moment. In other words, what they shared was the fact that each could recall a problematic or otherwise moving event much earlier in life than one might have thought relevant to a career decision made later on—sometimes, in fact, decades later.

It took a few years of part-time work to complete follow-up interviews with doctors, but I was eventually able to speak with more than forty physicians about these early experiences and their career decisions, and to confirm my findings in multiple interview and informal settings. About halfway through the interview process, what clearly emerged was *not* that one needs to commit oneself early in life if one is to have the stamina for potentially difficult professional work—that is, that one had, as it were, to be "born" into the profession—but that these early experiences had been important *because they were destabilizing*. Repeatedly the doctors I spoke with threaded their interview narratives with descriptions of how they had been moved, sometimes even against what seemed their preferences, by an illness encounter that they would remember again and again—some moment when they saw themselves beginning to be influenced, even changed, in the face of a sensitizing and even trying moment. This distinction—between deciding early and being sensitized early—is subtle, but it is also crucial; for it allows us to focus both on what really matters in these experiences and on why we have thus far failed to address with much success the problem of how we get medical students to commit themselves to working independently, and often alone, in remote areas. Their views of how they changed, we will see, also provide us with some useful insights into the nature of human transformation in contemporary life.

Perhaps most obvious in these interviews was the shared perception that early experiences were important because they had been, if you will, "inoculating." That nervous hospital volunteer standing helplessly observing some uncomfortable procedure had actually been moved in a way the importance of which would only be validated by a professional decision some years—perhaps many years—later. Moreover, whether these early experiences had been good or bad, what was more significant was the fact that they were destabilizing enough to produce a degree of sensitivity. What these experiences gave rise to, in other words, was a limited destabilization that was powerful enough to induce some transformation. They were powerful catalysts, but not so powerful as to be wholly defeating, inoculating but not immobilizing.

While today's practicing physicians may scoff at what teenagers actually get out of, let alone contribute to, clinical settings, we heard again and again from mature physicians that these early experiences helped them to commit themselves to the local moral worlds of rural general practice—to choose rural practice even over and above the other institutionally based opportunities without which their less independent colleagues could not live happily. This fact was made clear by several dimensions of our findings. In particular, we were surprised to discover that while 80 percent of those surveyed said that their undergraduate colleges and universities had prepared them well for medical school, some one-third of them said that medical school did not prepare them to be primary-care practitioners, and a full 40 percent said that this training did not prepare them for work in a rural area. Medical schools, in other words, did a good job of continuing the system of rewards of the undergraduate institutions these doctors had attended, but the institutional values of medical school were for a significant percentage of these doctors incommensurable with rural practice.

Well, you might skeptically inquire, if 40 percent of the doctors engaged in primary-care work in a rural area think that their job consists of activities other than what they were trained for, then ought we not at least consider introducing some elective courses in our high schools and colleges that would help alert future doctors to the realities of the profession they anticipate entering? To explore this question, we held a symposium in 1991, at the small liberal arts college where I teach, on the undergraduate premedical curriculum and discovered among other things that many university-based doctors felt that rural doctors were wasting too much of their time with so-called "social work."[3] Putting aside for purposes of the present discussion this discrepancy in professional views, we at least need to ask ourselves why, as is clearly the case, we are failing to focus on making possible such early experiences when we know them to be seminal?[4]

Part of the answer is easily uncovered: that mature doctor who invites a teenager to shadow her may never know how important the event truly was; for if you ask doctors immediately after students have such experiences about the outcome of that first encounter, their answers are fairly predictable: "Oh, it was good, but send him back when he has some clinical skills and he'll get much more out of seeing patients." With an American population that moves on average once every three years, the chances become increasingly less likely that the teenager in question will appear at that same doctor's door twenty or thirty years later to express his thanks. Furthermore, if he does return, the physician who made the event possible may by that time recall it only dimly, thinking instead that the polite words are just that. Moreover, and this situation is especially insidious in academic settings populated by "important" people, talking about the experience of relatively immature teenagers lacks the glamour and panache that comes with the evocation of startling human tragedy.[5] Is it any wonder that such events go unnoticed?

So permit me to turn to a second example that, I think, isolates the transformational nature of our problem and offers some clear explanation as well of the decision-making process upon which these students had embarked. Here, I have chosen an example that also, for comparative purposes, has a clinical fix, but one that, because it is more distressing, also brings the consequences of these destabilizing events into higher relief.

Many years ago, as a fellow of the Harvard Medical School, I approached the dean of students about internship opportunities currently being exploited by medical students that might be made available to college undergraduates. After initially stating—for reasons already outlined herein—that younger students would be unprepared for the clinical settings in which medical school students worked, she went to her file cabinet and withdrew some information on a homeless hospital in central London that was as eclectic as it was successful. In this hospital, the cost of treating tuberculosis, for instance, had been cut in half by stimulating among the homeless compliance to antibiotic treatments of their disease. Even more shocking, I learned that a year after discharge half of those treated at this facility had remained in the new housing that social services had located for them. Given that most homeless shelters have an approximate 98 percent recidivism rate—that is to say, a "revolving door"—keeping half of those treated off the streets signaled a remarkable achievement by any standard.[6] More curious still was the fact that the Oxford-educated doctors who cared for the homeless lived themselves in the facility.

Though the hospital had never had undergraduates before, when I met its director a few weeks later, he agreed to my initially sending a few students to see how they would fare in such a challenging setting. He too was curious about whether these younger individuals might be more willing to speak with the homeless than recently trained medical students eager to demonstrate their knowledge and authority. In fact, though several neophyte doctors had had excellent experiences at the hospital, others had considered it a good way of getting to London—a "soft" assignment in an excellent location. How many recently trained doctors, after all, had the patience and interest to spend long periods of time trying to extract a clinical history from an unbathed, aggressive patient with alcohol dementia? We all, moreover, were well aware of the then-recent studies that exposed the embarrassing fact that medical students actually got *worse* at taking case histories—that is, at *listening*—through the course of their medical training—a fact largely attributed to their being conditioned to address the expectations of their professors rather than those of their patients whose cases it is their duty to work up and scrutinize (Good 1994:65ff).

Without going too deeply into the details, suffice it to say that I ended up studying this hospital over a period of some six years, during which time twenty-four of my undergraduates spent one month each observing caregiving, shadowing doctors, and befriending patients.[7] For some students, the experience was deeply transforming. Upon their return to the United States, seven of them stated that the experience had been unequivocally cathartic. They used words like "deeply moving," "unforgettable," and "life-changing" to describe what had happened to them. But the other seventeen had more complex reactions.[8] Except for perhaps one individual who found the environment—no doubt, justifiably—too demanding, they would say things like the following: "being there was very important, but it took me most of the month to figure out what I was doing"; or "there were no guidelines given for how I should behave, and this made me feel uncomfortable until quite late in my stay"; or finally, "it all came together for me in the last three or four days"—a statement that was almost always followed by "if you could just add more structure to the internship, I think that future students would get more out of it early on."

Of course, in an age of political correctness made more prescriptive through our complete commodifying of higher education, that is exactly what we do—march out and overinscribe everything. At my college, for example, every single student evaluation (some thousand or more of them by the time one reaches a tenure review) are pored over by scrutinizing reappointment committees, and unlike when I was a student and course readings were often not sorted out until we met one another and discussed our interests on the first day of class, syllabi are produced months in advance for every course and kept on file to assure that there is continuity both across the curriculum and in one's own teaching habits. The academic version of "providing more structure" results in such a setting in the angry student who rebels at any faculty demand for work that is, as we say, not on the syllabus.

These experiences are familiar enough to anyone teaching today that I do not need to belabor them, but I do want to note the fact that the review process means that academics are rewarded and punished largely on information gathered through evaluations that are filled out by students in the final days of classes and that such procedures are common to how as a society we now live. Consumer statisticians, for instance, harass purchasers for first impressions of products.[9] Even hospitals now send satisfaction surveys home with their nauseatingly large bills. In the case of the homeless hospital, in other words, our college would have come down pretty hard on us were they, rather than a more forgiving nonprofit organization, footing the bill.[10] But they were not funding these experiences, and so we did not find ourselves under pressure to produce the requisite educational commodity that would, in turn, produce the future opening of alumni wallets. Instead, our independence allowed us to do something very different.

For the two years following these internships, we invited students back to ask basically the same questions about what the experience had meant and, in so doing, uncovered some interesting trends. In every case, what we found after six months was that the student who said, "It was really good, but give us more structure," now said something like this: "It was a really good experience; I'm still not sure what it meant to me, but I know it was important." In other words, the unsettled first interview—characterized by the need for more structure and the unstated accusation that "I didn't feel comfortable *and it's your fault*"—now had a more measured tone. By this time, some veterans were already indicating that the experience had been deeply transforming—a feeling that all of them would eventually come to express, but *at differing lengths of time*, over the coming years. What clearly was happening—albeit individually and often over several years—was that each volunteer was engaged in what anthropologists used to call a "rite of passage." This is not an exotic rite per se, but a series of connected events in which an initial destabilizing moment—an "inversion" of everyday expectations—places one in a condition of "liminality," a symbolic location "betwixt and between," to recall Victor Turner (1964), what we once were and what we will next become.

Now, before readers accuse me of being an unreformed structuralist, I should emphasize that understanding this truism of human growth has nothing to do with endorsing or not endorsing structuralism, though, I suppose, the articulation of any kind of movement from A to B risks that label. At the same time, it does not take much imagination to recognize several truisms:

1) that an inversion of expectations places one on alert;
2) that the feeling of being vulnerable to the outside (that uncertainty, threat, stress, and so on) allows one to recognize the possibility of being changed by an external agent;
3) that the sensitizing (the inoculating) one is subjected to facilitates the act of filling in the blanks of, as it were, one's self-portrait; and
4) that once completed, this new picture of oneself gets presented and verified socially.

Understanding change in its simplest form, in other words, asks only that we acknowledge how a self recognizes that it has become something identifiably "new."

So, what made our rural doctors dedicated and our hospital volunteers reflective were, in short, *inversions*—that is, destabilizations—that once resolved allowed individuals to recognize that they had been irrevocably *changed* by the stimulation of an unsettling moment. This idea is not anthropological high theory, but simple common sense. Indeed, unlike that peculiar cultural phenomenon called depth psychology, these are no more or less than basic processes through which humans across the world and throughout time have acknowledged some alteration in identity.

Moreover, these are also *not*, I should hasten to add, rites of passage enacted in terms that would necessarily have pleased Arnold van Gennep (1909). What distinguished the transformations of these individuals from the changes characteristic of more "traditional" group rites was the varying lengths of time it took every student intern to complete her private becoming. For each student who returned immediately transformed by the experience, there were two or three who might not complete this change for a year, or two, or fifteen—a fact that takes us back to what happened when that seventeen-year-old future doctor stood nervously observing the examination of some patient for the first time.

Because nothing here speaks to the kind of psychological discourse on self-help to which we have all grown accustomed, we might justifiably ask, if this is how all of us change, why are we so unable to perceive the importance of these processes as they are unfolding?[11] Why are we apparently so ignorant of the need to make possible such experiences? Why, alas, do we remain so incapable of facilitating them? Why, to put it bluntly, do we actually seem so determined to promote the opposite—to limit so much the initial destabilization that we end up denying the possibility for change at its very outset?

Old-time structuralists would say that a fundamental feature of ritual is to mark time (E. Leach 1961). If we have no inversion at a solstice or equinox—if we have no Mardi Gras—it is inevitable that we should come to fear these inversions as *only* destabilizing. Time, they would argue, is a perceived, not an absolute thing. And because it is perceived, the past is much more than a memory. We don't, for instance, need quantum mechanics to see time as influenced by perception. Tonight, if I am lucky, I may witness a meteor shower that took place in the eighteenth century. We think, so to speak, that returning to the past is a feat restricted to science fiction, to witchcraft, or to delirium, even when a look at the heavens on any clear night can easily prove otherwise, alerting us to the empirical possibilities of looking into the past.

Time, our structuralists would then argue, is in fact so much a matter of perception that we can lose sight of its measuring function if we fail to use it regularly as a measure.[12] Indeed, the anthropologist of yesteryear would be much more willing to accept the mutability of unstructured time (for example, Gell 1992) than would his postmodern colleague who needs to see current strategies for negotiating chaotic time as part of something that in some traditional temporal evolution follows modernity. Indeed, our resurrected structuralist would say that a failure to respect the fact that time must be ritually marked is our clearest indicator that perceiving its heuristic utility may now be beyond our grasp.

Life on the Long Trail

Thus far, I have compared the profound personal changes I have witnessed to experiences characteristic of life-transforming collective rites, but I have only intimated the ways in which such rites might be fundamentally different from what we experience today. Permit me now to be specific.

To say that the sequences of today's individual transformations differ from other contexts and settings where groups of individuals define themselves through collective rites is to imply that the human need for collective cohesion is circumstantial. However, it is also to imply that the importance of the element of *time* is today underestimated. Here postmodernism has done much to promulgate the notion of temporal flexibility, even if it has done less to acknowledge the consequences of its own argument for our ability to communicate at all with one another.[13] Some modern-day transitions occur in a day, a week, or a month, while others of us respond to the same stimuli only over a year, or two, or ten. Setting aside for the moment the question of how any of us end up communicating at all in such a world, the consequences of this variability for our embodied understanding of change can be profound.[14] Where we once, perhaps, moved from one social estate to the next through a carefully orchestrated event, by the time one today actually reaches a place where a new identity is integrated, years may easily separate us from the visceral sweating, the ecstatic joy, and the *desire*—from the *shared* moments—that are so essential to the bodily awareness of being transformed.[15] This, in my view, is one major reason why depth psychology and psychiatric pharmacology fail so consistently and so miserably. Because they fear the potentially negative outcome of stress, they in general seek to limit it well in advance of its becoming catalytic.

Far more damaging, though, is that the length of time sometimes required to facilitate an individual's own private passage also has the effect of undermining one's ability to acknowledge that any transformation is processual—that is, to know over time that one is in the midst of it all. Our anxieties, that is, become extended over time in various behaviors that we find wholly unhealthy because their potential for resolution is withheld from us at every turn. Here, the behavioral inversions characteristic of change become enough conditions of everyday life that their prevalence amounts to what we see as "psychological incapacities." This extended nature of contemporary change is probably also accountable for the modern connection between creative genius and depression—why, for instance, so many Nobel laureates are clinically depressed and why in general psychoanalysis does so well as a fashionable consumer commodity despite its poor track record. The ecstatic joy or fear of a cathartic event (that is, the inchoate nature of its stress) gets normalized (that is, habituated) over longer and longer durations and, in turn, becomes interpreted as the pathological behavior of an attention-deficit, obsessive-compulsive, manic-depressive, delusional personality who is at best "borderline," if not altogether quite mad.[16] Here the deep satisfaction of a desire fulfilled is undermined by an attenuated reflection on one's inability to achieve it. The thought that one's patience might one day be rewarded gets replaced by the realization that one has been habituated to indolence.

Finally, and perhaps most troubling of all, our confusion about this process, our anxieties about ourselves, and our perceptions about the rapidly changing world around us all have the effect of causing us to think that we are constantly changing when, at the level of personal development, we are undoubtedly *slowing down*. That person whose rite of passage begins while shadowing a doctor at the age of seventeen and ends with the decision to enter medical school at the age of forty may well only have one such transformation in a lifetime. Whether you say that this slowing down occurs because of how "out of touch" we are today with our emotions (Napier 2003), or because the world is moving faster than any of us can possibly make good psychological use of, the bottom line is that individuals caught up in such emotional alienation and instability cannot help but perceive change wrongly.

Compared to a premodern Hindu, for instance, for whom life is characterized after adolescence by a householder stage and its concomitant professional activism, a time of seclusion, and a final relinquishing—the "abandonment"— of earthly responsibilities in favor of a spiritual life, our doctor who begins practice at thirty or thirty-five and ends it three decades later in idle retirement can look relatively uninfluenced by life—that is, untransformed by that remarkable experience called living. And what defense does he have to reverse this tendency? Well, in fact, not much of one—especially if, as is so often the case, the transformational process occurs so slowly as to escape his very notice.

So what can he do to recover some contact with his senses? In lieu of his alienation from time, he does what all good aliens do: he either becomes a demonic force—because those "out of time" have always been in the position of being "born under a bad sign," that is, always doing bad when they try to do good[17]—or he accepts his alienation and decides instead to write about it. This is, of course, why writing today has such health benefits for those who practice it—because in the absence of any physical sense of transformational closure, one can at least re-create the sense of continuous change through narratively structuring that which would otherwise have remained inchoate.

Having elsewhere discussed this at the level of embodiment (Napier 2003), I will here restrict myself to two (startling) health-related examples that would seem to confirm this conclusion. One is the rise of what Pollock has called physician "training tale" (Pollock 1996)—that is, the recent and unprecedented proliferation of books in which doctors describe their passage through medical training and the inhumanity of the medical schools in which they are trained. Here an entire genre has appeared in which up-and-coming doctors claim to be writing, as so many academics now do, from the peripheries about their perceived professional alienation. The second is the recent discovery by experimental psychologists (for example, Pennebaker and Graybeal 2001) that codifying a destabilizing event to which one has been subjected, by writing about that event retrospectively, helps to facilitate its psychological closure (Adams 1986). In both of these cases, we see how the "writing of passage" becomes for authors a "health benefiting"—that is, a *closure determining*—activity because writing offers a means of resolving an unsettling event whose visceral meaning has been jeopardized by time. As Foucault has aptly remarked of "self writing," "the constraint that the presence of others exerts in the domain of conduct, writing will exert in the domain of the inner impulses of the soul" (1997a:208). Writing, that is, constrains the soul at the same time as it provides the soothing closure for an ancient visceral moment that one failed to act upon.

"There once upon a time was a man who was partly Dave," wrote John Lennon in his aptly titled book, *In His Own Write*. Closure and writing, now perhaps more than ever, appear to function as devices for Dave's becoming less "partly." I only need reflect momentarily on how the vast majority of my students combine the spiritually uplifting activity of hiking the Long Trail with the act of journal writing to get a frightening look into the current epidemic.

What I mean by this is the prolonged ritual activity in which writing about one's failure to achieve emotional closure—that is, to know something bodily—gives way to a literary activity through which one rationalizes long after that catalytic moment of dissociation the visceral road not taken. In the end, one may well be tempted to inquire of a friend where one might "go to surrender"; for in all of these examples we employ the process of writing to institutionalize our alienation from institutions, as if resolving one's alienation narratively were the major prerequisite for gaining membership in what can rightly be called our "amodern" world. If, that is, "you opt out of the exact science, then the human sciences, then traditional philosophy, then the sciences of language, and you hunker down in your forest—then you will indeed feel a tragic loss. But what is missing is you yourself, not the world" (Latour 1993:66)!

Yes, the unexpected effects of not describing another's liminality can be made palpable under extreme conditions, but who will put themselves to such a test? In fact, what we witness is the exact opposite. Those who habitually revisit another's misfortune through narrative description may themselves feel compelled to write not because they can share the experiences of their subjects, but because they are once removed from those experiences, or, if not removed, at least resigned to the static nature of life as they live it. Is it any wonder then that authors who write about the transcendental experiences of others so regularly are met by indifference when their writings are presented to those whose lives they have described—even, it seems, when they cannot be accused of that "unseemly eagerness to exploit the victims' suffering for polemical advantage"?

What, in other words, needs to be emphasized repeatedly is not merely that we may be changing more slowly today while feeling that modernity has swept us away, but that the often extremely unhealthy nature of our false liminality leaves us with years of psychologizing about our feelings of inadequacy and ambivalence. Looked at this way, the flexible nature of the postmodern condition—where we shift identities as we adjust to the chaos of transnational life—may be understood less as the consequence of so many novel social encounters than as the outcome of not recognizing the lengthy liminality that dominates a world filled with exceedingly retarded transformations.

Why else, for instance, is our popular culture so frightened by change—concerned not only to defuse stress as early as we can pump Ritalin into the human animal "in the gate," but given to fantasizing in our media and in our private lives about all manner of hysterically transformed bionic terminators? Where are the positive, creative examples—one might justifiably ask of a willful giving over of the self—that taking of chance that in times long since past was the stuff of making love and of enjoying its risks?

Time Out of Time; or, Go Jump in a Lake

I began this chapter with two examples of human change whose transformative qualities seem, in retrospect, so self-evident as hardly to bear mentioning.[18] It would be odd to listen to the narratives about personal growth offered by the primary-care doctors I interviewed, or to the students' explanations of their internships among the homeless, without sensing the veracity of what they say, and without recognizing that their experiences were exemplary of the sort of change that in other settings might have taken place within the framework of a rite of passage. What we observe in these cases, that is, are powerful forms of human growth, but not of a kind made familiar to us through the claims of depth psychologists. In the cases I have described, change is the outcome of a destabilizing moment and not, at least initially, the result of a demonstrable control over one's destiny. This destabilization can be labeled with a variety of descriptors, but what is more important than its name is the fact that it takes the form of some dissociative state.[19]

What I mean here is that if one sets aside the fact that the transformations I have described for doctors and for my student volunteers are couched in each individual's narrative, and if one adjusts for the fact that their transformations take place over variable periods of time, the actual processes of these most deeply altering experiences look much more like passage rites than they do the sort of meditative ponderings we associate with depth psychology. Because, in other words, these events appear to corroborate the idea that dissociation is a universal aspect of change, we must accept the degree to which dissociation is central to *any* discourse about transformation. This is a conclusion whose truth is easily evidenced, as we have argued, in the similarity between illness experience and religious experience—where in both cases we witness the profound effects of destabilizations that are identical in all respects, save their outcomes. Positive destabilizations, as in the moment of spiritual "enlightenment," are the essence of religious experience while negative destabilizations are the stuff of both physical and mental illness. Can too much be made of the similarity? Maybe, but I doubt it; for one only need examine the degree to which an illness in one setting can be perceived as a gift in another to see how close these often dissimilar phenomena are.

A description from a friend who has experienced seizures makes the point more eloquently than any argument could: "I never thought of this 'illness' as a negative aspect of my life. I've found over the years that it was actually quite an amazing experience. When I was having a seizure, and even today when I faint, it is one of the most soothing and peaceful places that I know or have ever experienced. And this is only to awake to people staring, yelling, and at times slapping you in fear of something worse happening." Indeed, how many times throughout history has this "illness" been called divine? And why should we not respect the fact that such events can have either or both meanings, depending on their context? After all, change is not transformational unless a bad outcome is as possible as a good one—unless at the moment of being moved by a destabilizing thing, we are unable to resolve our uncertainty about the consequences of that risk which is essential for change. How, to put it rhetorically, can one know that one has changed unless one accepts the altering impact of having been overcome by someone or something?

Considered thus, we can readily illustrate how all narratives of change are characterized by some initial destabilization, a leveling out of individuality, that becomes the catalyst for a deep feeling of uncertainty, alienation, and liminalty—even of being overtaken or possessed by a threatening or enchanting outside agent. This experience of extreme psychological ambivalence—variable though its duration may be today—would have, in another time or place, constituted the central, or sacred, part of a transformational rite. The discomfort may have been no less then than now, but our contemporary absence of faith in the positive dimensions of stress would have been mitigated by empirical evidence that validated the possibility that stress could be highly beneficial as well as destructive. The contemporary obsession with horror films, like the eighteenth-century obsession with Gothic novels, may in this way be read as a broadly held distrust of being transformed by an outsider with whom we do not know how to make love. Is it any wonder then that we tend to see stress as a largely unhealthy, if not wholly debilitating, thing? Where today are all of the romances involving Terminators?

The argument—that the temporal extension of transformations causes a separation of intellect from visceral awareness—seems then worthy of some consideration; for in extending these transformational encounters over several years, we inevitably separate the power of the emotional moment from its long-term rationalization. We take ourselves, that is, away from the embodied understanding of what might be possible and move, instead, toward a less physical awareness—the stuff of intellectual ruminating. What may have been a cathartic, even religious inversion of the everyday becomes over time the ongoing fabric of our psychological disabilities, and our hope for creating something new gets similarly warped into a "pathological manifestation"—one that we learn to describe through the controlled rhetoric of depth psychology.

If slowing down then is a process of separating embodiment from knowledge, how much have our social institutions contributed to the process of learning about the effects of reflection on extended forms of change? To be honest, they have not been terribly helpful. In fact, one might without much work successfully argue that these very modern institutions have so homogenized the concept of living that nobody could expect them to be anything other than emotionally restricting.

While artists may by disposition find it easier than most to criticize the emotionless pragmatism of those who do well in institutional settings, perhaps the calculated absence of risk within the academy itself incites the most acerbic criticism. As Jean Dubuffet, the well-known artist and champion of the outsider, puts it,

Professors are grown-up schoolchildren, schoolchildren who, once their school days were over left school through one door only to return through another, like military men who *reenlist*. They are schoolchildren who, instead of aspiring to an adult life, that is to say a creative life, cling to this schoolchild's stance, a stance which is passively receptive, like a sponge. The creative spirit is as opposed as possible to that of the professor. Artistic (or literary) creation has more in common with all other forms of creation (in the most common domains of business, the crafts or any type of work, manual or otherwise) than it has with the purely conformational attitude of the professor, who is by definition animated by no creative taste and must give his praise indifferently to all that *won acceptance* in the long developments of the past. The professor is the expert who indexes, who endorses, who confirms all that won acceptance, from wherever and whenever these works originated. Renaissance architects scorned the gothic style, and the architects of Art Nouveau scorned those of the Renaissance, but the professor celebrates them all at once in his impassioned discourse for his heart is filled with enchantment for the accepted, with eagerness to applaud the accepted wherever it may be seen. (1988:13)

Though to those of us occupying university posts this may appear a harsh and aggressive characterization,[20] it would not induce strong objections were it not also to contain some germ of truth; for what institutional creativity can be evidenced when so-called intellectuals preoccupy themselves with feathering their nests while their supposedly powerful administrative overlords reward complacency and conformity?

If academics are as incapable of individual action as Dubuffet suggests, then it stands to reason that the institutions that they enslave themselves to are far less powerful than we generally believe them to be. If, in other words, institutions attempt to succeed by getting everyone to do the same things—that is, by inducing conformity—then it also stands to reason (as Foucault discovered only in his later work[21]) that institutions will, when left to their own entropic devices, bring themselves down without assistance. Let us not forget here that our word *normal* means "rule" or "measure" (Canguilhem [1966] 1989:239-40)—that the worlds in which norms really matter are governed by institutions that will always attempt to define standards of acceptability in exceedingly narrow terms. Talking about the powers of institutions, in other words, is not only a way of defending our complacency, but a coded way of excusing the weaknesses of those of us who cannot live without such "normalcy."

What then of these institutions? If they have even tricked our deeply contemplative postmodernists into thinking that the "new reality" is a rapidly changing one, why is it that the same old faces seem to inhabit all of those endowed dusty chairs of intellectual conformity? Moreover, how has it come to pass that we think of ourselves as constantly changing when the institutionalized world at large is so obviously characterized by entropy? Whether this retreat from transformational encounters is the result of the unsettling nature of contemporary life or a deep fear of the alien (Napier 2003), one thing is certain. Such questions will not be answered in the pages of any book, though they may be embodied in the fulfillment that comes of accepting risk, of acknowledging desire, and of sustaining not a little bit of optimism in a world more accustomed to its opposite.

Chapter 5
The All-White Elephant

> *We deplore or laugh at those who try to arm themselves against the apocalypse, but we arm ourselves emotionally against the onslaught of everyday life.*
>
> —*Lasch*, The Minimal Self

Are You Experienced?

> *Fame is the spur that the clear spirit doth raise*
> *(That last infirmity of noble mind)*
>
> —*Milton*, Lycidas, *70–71*

Not long ago I was (yes, absentmindedly) standing at the checkout counter of the Yale University Co-op in downtown New Haven, Connecticut. As I waited for my turn to pay, I noticed that the person in front of me in line was seriously handicapped. She made her purchase, and with some difficulty, started for the door. About to take my merchandise, the clerk—a young, black businessman in this whiter-than-white place—noticed her need, suddenly dropped his task, and ran to the door to hold it for her. A few moments later he returned, trying as best he could to regain his composure and resume his routine without drawing attention to his momentary absence.

But I couldn't resist. Being who I am, I had to tell him that I thought his politeness commendable. I said something unimaginative like "that was very kind of you." However, before I could regain *my* distance, he raised his head, looked right at me and said, "You see, my younger brother was murdered by a gunman in this town, and I feel I have to do something, because I know that he is forever gone."

In fact, the conversation continued well after these words, for he was noticeably taken aback by my being as ruled by my own compulsions as he clearly was by his. I have other memories of our brief encounter, but I mention what I have because the incident brought into high relief the emotive disjunction between the relatively mannered lives of all of those seriously well-educated folks in white lab coats at the nearby medical school, and this guy who, in light of his misery, had to work hard just to look good behind his counter. The incident also brought forward another disjunction—this one being between an institutionalized system of shared value on the one hand, and a personalized domain of private, homemade meaning that this local response to tragedy represented.

So, am I rendering his experience exotically? You bet I am. Because no matter how much I may "feel" for him, he remains behind his counter, while I end up writing this very opinionated book. In fact, he is moved by his experience into a domain of meaning that I would in no way wish to relive. To say that such experiences—even several of them—have brought me "closer" to New Haven street life would be hypocritical in the extreme. And to offer them up in literary form as "stories" from my "fieldwork" among the socially disenfranchised would be singularly elitist. I want no part of what he experienced, but I am *moved* by his optimism nonetheless. I am not, in other words, soliciting your sympathies here any more than he did mine. I am only asking you to acknowledge the idea that reality—the experience of the present—changes in sudden ways that can make an obsession about either the "lived worlds" of those nearby university people, or all of the theories that justify the complacency of institutional life seem, um, trivial.

This is not to denigrate directly any individual's institutional loyalty or to belittle the human passion for routine, but merely to note that the glamorization of the everyday—disguised as it so often seems to be in a cloak of false humility—induces both an inflated sense of self-importance and that concomitant disinterest in real difference that is myopia's favored bedfellow.

To extend the argument, one might say that it is easy within a bureaucracy to feign a respect for the diversities of the everyday when the obedience of drones sustains a prevailing hierarchy within which one is richly rewarded. Such complacency, after all, accounts for the fact that most academic departments more represent priesthoods than environments conducive to intellectual exchange; for the existence of independent thought within an institution is almost always inversely proportionate in my experience to its intellectual reputation. It is what the French mean by the term *équipe*. Indeed, in the many academic posts I have filled throughout my career, I have experienced no more real freedom than I did while teaching at a small parochial college with a less than stellar reputation.

You may, in other words, say all you want when you speak about narrative voice, or the need for a fuller account, a thicker description of the subtle complexities of the everyday. But until the day—god forbid—when I am able to know this man's life, he will thankfully remain very exotic to me. Until that time I will unashamedly stand in awe and admiration of his resilience, his hope, and (how can I say it?) his humanity.

So why then not label this event by dwelling on it "thickly," turning it into moral capital—a nice story—with which to assuage my own guilt and that of my reader? Here one must remember that the notion of thick description was not an invention put to work by ethnographers after Geertz (1973), but of literary theorists in search of a way of fusing multiple experiences into singular descriptions. The very concept, in other words, is the outcome of an attempt, especially by Henry James, to show how one's repeated exposure to a series of related events induces, to paraphrase Aristotle, the effect of a single experience. For James, the story that lacked such depth of experience was—as, indeed, he considered American culture itself—too "thin" (Lentricchia 1990:333). It was the humbly rendered depth of experience that made a story compelling, not the volume of narrative details that allowed an author to own it.

Thus, even though nice stories are what everybody likes—at times being emblematic, even compelling—when exquisitely rendered to the inexperienced, they can also be deterrents to that more difficult task called living. Yes, everyone likes a good story, but few of us can see in our own daily living the abnormally good form—the artful disclosures—that words make possible. That lengthy, rich description is, in other words, nothing more nor less than the exploration of that artificial convention called literature—a thing much the world is denied the pleasure of knowing, a figment of life reduced to an inscribed gesture. Think only for a moment of the many subjects of the best anthropological writing who themselves have not read—or even cared much for reading—their own "stories" and one gets the picture of this reality in its starker formulation.

Stories work miracles among those cloned on academic living—that is, for those who have been shaped by, and cannot live without, the acquisition of diplomas, awards, professorships, and other such badges of conformity—but nice stories are far from the only means by which humans convey meaning and otherwise socially interact (for example, Stoller 1989b). Sometimes stories mean less than, say, incantations—or songs, or the following of prescriptions, or the taste of certain foods—to those whose lives are otherwise defined.

What role then does the everyday play in understanding things apparently exotic? How do we sufficiently disarm ourselves against the onslaught of everyday institutional life to recognize the potential that real difference presents? For James, making art out of life required that one transpose the everyday into a domain influenced by the refinements of the exotic, for without some acknowledgement of the exotic one could neither structure one's emotions in the face of repeated displays of human sentiment—that is, formulate good judgments about the "everyday"—nor comprehend why those paradigmatic cases appear so "thick" to us in the first place. Why else, after all, did Henry James end up in England?

If, in other words, we remain content with glamorizing our own participation in, and knowledge of, common things, we shall surely just as easily excuse our ignorance of difference by mistaking that ignorance for what we believe to be some form of honesty, pretentious though it may be. If, to put it on the personal level, I cannot bring myself to risk an encounter with difference, then I will surely do my best to ignore, if not actively to wreck, the legitimacy of yours. If you like, you may well read this tendency as a primary motivator of contemporary academic life.

So, while it may not be initially obvious, there is a deep reason for sustaining some curiosity about the exotic. This reason being that if we not only glorify the everyday, but also trivialize and stigmatize that which is genuinely different (Goffman 1963), we become defenseless in attempting to know how to construct a response to the unknown. It is here where academics are just as culpable as the evangelists they designate. As Stanley Fish put it in a recent article about the irreconcilabilities of Islamic fundamentalism and the so-called postmodern democracy,

> The problem is not that there is no universal—the universal, the absolutely true, exists, and I know what it is. The problem is that you know, too, and that we know different things, which puts us right back where we were . . . armed with universal judgments that are irreconcilable, all dressed up and nowhere to go for an authoritative adjudication.
>
> What to do? Well, you do the only thing you can do, the only honest thing: you assert that your universal is the true one, even though your adversaries clearly do not accept it, and you do not attribute their recalcitrance to insanity or mere criminality—the desired public categories of condemnation—but to the fact, regrettable as it may be, that they are in the grip of a set of beliefs that is false. And there you have to leave it, because the next step, the step of proving the falseness of their beliefs to everyone, including those in their grip, is not a step available to us as finite situated human beings. We have to live with the knowledge of two things: that we are absolutely right and that no generally accepted measure exists by which our rightness can be independently validated. (2002:37)

In this respect, religious fundamentalism and contemporary academic life may actually share more than one might think; because for Fish the problem is not one of extreme cultural relativism—of saying that there are different (radical) strokes for different folks and my thick description will make you appreciate that "other" view—but of the demonizing of deep otherness in favor of one's own private universal, "a general perspective that claims to be universal and has the advantage of disturbing no one because it is at once both safe and empty" (38). And no matter how politically conservative one's orientation, the problem is not made simpler by the assumption that globalization and progress are one and the same (Stiglitz 2002:5): "Those who vilify globalization too often overlook its benefits. But the proponents of globalization have been, if anything, even more unbalanced. To them, globalization (which typically is associated with accepting triumphant capitalism, American style) *is* progress; developing countries must accept it, if they are to grow and to fight poverty effectively."

Of course, it is difficult to imagine another way of living if your fear of acknowledging difference is combined with your sense of guilt about perhaps taking too much of what the world is made of. Without citing all of the statistics about American overconsumption (Schor 1998), one must remember that hiding one's gluttony in humanitarian diatribe does not reduce the sublimated guilt that should result from stashing your wealth—under a pillow, in the Cayman Islands, in a summer-home investment, or in a lengthy curriculum vitae— any more than ignoring diverging views of what moves the world advances your understanding of why other people behave as they do. Neither modernity nor globalization, in other words, does very much in themselves to make us less culturally myopic.

It is then in their shared desire for global ideological homogeneity that fundamentalists, political ideologues, and many academics so often cross paths, because all three are sometimes involved in "an effort to narrow the range of what can be said to a rote . . . discourse that is a form of cheerleading rather than serious thought" (Fish 2002:38). Cornered by convention, we find ourselves either disbelieving another's familiarity with deep human difference, or having waited so long to acknowledge that difference, we jump on the bandwagon of whatever notion appears to be ruling the day. In the first case, we dismiss difference outright, calling the writing of those who attend to it "sensational", while in the second we overstate it—that is, treat it heroically once its presence in our lives appears irrevocable—which, by the way, is why I stand by my view of our more "important" Institutions of Higher Something or Other as increasingly restrictive.

The problem is not then between, for example, Islam and the rest of the world, or between anthropologists who really "know" about human experience and those who do not. The problem is one of recognizing the limitations placed on certainty by self-censorship—by the internalization of whichever beliefs we might otherwise have discussed, but which now exist in a private domain of socially and morally underdeveloped fantasy. This situation presents the real dilemma with political correctness today: none of our cherished beliefs, let alone our private prejudices, have been socially challenged or tried in any "thick" experiential sense. Thus understood, we begin to see that the limitations under which we function are no less prevalent in our own academic institutions than they are in Islam, or Christianity, or any other worldview— especially when that worldview is enough committed to its system of beliefs to be characterized by nonbelievers as "fundamental"; for the desire to demonize is far more emotionally attractive to, and thus has more power for, the anxious believer (religious or academic) than the attraction of an abstract and emotionless form of inquiry. Witness, for instance, the rudeness of so many college professors in professional settings and you will see the similarities coldly.

The fear of one's own shallowness then not only causes each of us to deny the exotic, but to limit our capacity to accept basic difference. This self-sanctioning we sense because the anxiety caused by self-censorship is the outcome of having closed the door to difference far too prematurely, whether this closing takes place in New Delhi or in New York. In former times, such self-censorship was a feature of patrician sentiment, or, say, of misplaced chivalry in which we politely decline to contest openly just about everything. Today the self-censoring intellectual more resembles the freeze-dried winter orange that tempts us in the market—young and new-looking, yet internally dry, lifeless, and entirely without taste. But unlike that atrophied orange, the residual acidity that remains in the pulp gives way not only to indigestion, but also to a basic fear of alien substances in general.

And what are the effects of these tendencies on human behavior? In the face of this fear, we oscillate between the worshiping of those few heroes whose reputations appear indisputable while neglecting to value just about everyone else. This is why so many "advanced" civilizations are obsessed with canons that make "importance" an end in its own right—why we make heroes of one or two artists or writers while neglecting the many creative and talented individuals living in our midst. As R. D. Laing once taunted about the shallowness of American academic psychology,

I mean who is a great *American* philosopher? Well, the greatest American philosopher is Mark Twain, in his essays, Emerson, William James, Pierce and Dewey. But the whole thing gets terribly thinned down when—what a turning of the wine into the thinnest, thinnest milk trash—you compare Sartre or Camus with Abe Maslow. There's no tragedy, there's no irony. I can't imagine Nietzsche in America. But Rollo May is one of the best of them. There is no doubt of it.

Rollo said, "how would you like to stay [in California] if we could fix you up with a job?" so I had a few meetings with various people about staying in the Bay area and—this is another epitomizing example—a lunch was arranged with two Californian businessmen of some influence and wealth in California. . . . You have to be careful how you report this; they made it clear to me, this is an offer that if made to me I couldn't refuse. . . . yes, you will accept this, if we offer it to you. Do you want to meet the rector or president of Stanford University? Yes, I said, I have been dying to meet him all my life.

OK, so they give me a rap. Well, Stanford University—forget about Harvard and Yale and forget about the East Coast and forget about Princeton—Stanford is at this moment in time getting the cream of the crop . . . it is more difficult to get into Stanford University than anywhere else. They said they wouldn't want me to see undergraduates but after graduation—before they go out into the world—it would be very good for the best of them to be exposed to my mind. They added, you know, that "in the first year of Stanford they have the highest suicide rate of any university in America"—do you get the point? . . . Well, you are talking about getting jobs and obviously I'm not at Stanford just now, I'm here in the wilderness. (Mullan 1995:207)

Indeed, as Laing sarcastically acknowledged, whether we find ourselves at a given moment among the glorifiers or the detractors of a particular institution—in this case, Stanford University—is not in the end all that significant. What is significant is, first, the fact that we have arrived in whatever camp we inhabit because we have excused ourselves from having the courage to live outside of whichever institution pays our bills and, second, the fact that we have accomplished this allegiance by exaggerating and overstating the powers that these institutions have in controlling our behavior. It is interesting in this regard to see how those who have theorized about the ability of institutions to control us (for example, Foucault) have only later in life felt secure enough about the limits of institutional power—or their own reputation—to downgrade the extent to which institutions impose themselves on your will or mine. Though every Internet user may live in fear of the invasiveness of networks of technology, though he or she may be shocked by the prevalence of prejudice and pornography, it is the user, remember, who controls the power to that computer. The networks are, in other words, everywhere; but they need not influence us at all times unless we fully subscribe to them, and in so doing submit to their authority. This idea, after all, is the compliance to which Gramsci referred when speaking of hegemony.

So there is then an even more important reason for discussing the relationship between institutions we deem important and our denial of deep experiential difference. This being not only that we fail to recognize the limitations we exert on experiences by inscribing them, but in our love of inscribed emotion we fuel the tendency of modern social institutions to undermine the risk of actually living.

And what *do* we miss in our academically "fundamental" views about emotional depth? We miss, in the least, the pleasures of being thrilled by other modes of measuring experience—by, that is to say, the very thing that to us appears exotic. As Berger once wrote of "culturally deprived"—that is, formally uneducated—villagers of rural England,

a great deal of their experience—especially emotional and introspective experience—has to remain *unnamed* for them. . . . The easiest—and sometimes the only possible—form of conversation is that which concerns or describes action: that is to say action considered as technique or as procedure. It is then not the experience of the speakers which is discussed but the nature of an entirely exterior mechanism or event—a motorcar engine, a football match, a draining system or the workings of some committee. Such subjects, which preclude anything directly personal, supply the content of most of the conversations being carried on. (1997:99)

Note that Berger is not advocating that we measure the value of the peasants' perspectives multiculturally or by witnessing it in their emotionally deep narratives. *On the contrary*: to be rewarded by the creativity that uncertainty facilitates—for inscribing if anything certifies the uncertain—one cannot by definition devote one's life to defining another's experience, because creativity requires the acceptance that another's life might be richer and more humanly fulfilling than one's own. So much for all of the hand-holding that goes down for responsible emotion work in the classrooms of our up-market universities. Never mind the implications for ethnography.

For those of us who remain in love with "important" institutional conventions, the act of "writing it up" will always take precedence over "living it up" because we are encouraged by our allegiances to remain annoyed by, if not openly hostile toward, the unknown and possibly unknowable. This is why I have already described the act of ad hominem anthropological narrative—the exploitation of another's personal emotions in narrative description—as "the writing of passage," as the glorification of the author's own voice under the aegis of self-righteous indignation (see Chapter 3). This is also why the act of capturing in words has been so often understood—from Milton onward—as the handiwork of those who demonize what they cannot realize. Asks Eve of Satan in *Paradise Lost*, "What may this mean? Language of man pronounced / By tongue of brute, and human sense expressed?" What can it mean when the most frightening of alien beings reaches our deepest soul with words that men have failed to express? If nothing more, the alien informs us here in the most startling of ways that man has been asleep on the job and may actually have turned off the alarm clock; for he has done nothing if not subscribe to the academic version of what the British call "working to rule." The academic rule says that you cannot acknowledge what you do not know—easier then to argue that the unknown does not exist than to accept that one lives in fear of finding it.

The collusive nature of these destructive tendencies—of inflating the power of institutions while benefiting by our loyalty to them; of writing about the glorious everyday while patrolling another's claims on the exotic—is seen quite dramatically in the degree to which postmodern institutions induce collective complacency and reward mimicry. This is precisely why, as noted in the last chapter, medical schools are so successful at continuing the system of rewards of the undergraduate institutions from which they cull future doctors while at the same time doing rather poorly at preparing those future doctors for social domains other than those honored by their teaching faculties. Here let us remember that most research on doctor-patient relations is not conducted by primary caregivers but by medical professors who themselves may be incapable of surviving outside of the institutional networks that support their sometimes fragile egos, and whose institutions in turn increasingly depend upon the indirect costs of their research to pump up the insatiable corporate appetite for new buildings.[1]

So, what is the alternative to the bowing and scraping of those of us who have sold our freedom for a modicum of university status? By contrast with their institutionally dependent academic colleagues, most successful rural primary-care doctors survive by cultivating broader values that do not chain them professionally to conformist institutional networks. The more than two hundred rural doctors with whom I have worked are, in particular, not people who by and large place their fragile careers in front of their curiosity about what they do not know yet. They are, in other words, professional risk-takers—people willing enough to step beyond the confines of what their professional peers find rewarding (Donovan and Bain 2000). This explains why the rural doctor who is the focus of Berger's study spent so much time with his patients engaged in forms of understanding that seem only remotely "clinical." This explains why many rural doctors openly acknowledge their life-long interests in areas outside of what their university-based peers call "medicine"—why so many thrive on what the institutionalized would call "extracurricular activities." This explains why the illness encounters of many primary-care doctors can be so wholly embodied in nonclinical details that their "serious" university colleagues would deem irrelevant—why so much office time is devoted to talk about housing, finances, or the loves and tribulations of kin and distant relatives whose lives are now made all the more near by the self-awareness brought on by not feeling "right."

While institutional high-fliers may scoff at the sloppy nature of the rural primary-care doctor's clinical experiences, and while prescriptions on what can and cannot be considered "clinically relevant" become increasingly coercive (Satel 2000), the deep importance of a doctor's social integration can be most powerfully seen in its absence: asked by the compilers of a recent report on rural well-being to rank the four key elements that make up a community, residents of rural Scotland listed having a general practitioner (GP) as the number one defining feature, placing the GP ahead of a primary school (number two), a village hall (number three), and a post office (number four) as the very thing whose absence would undo them (McNicol 2002).

Set against the reality of doctors being increasingly trained to live under the bright lights of their medical research and teaching centers and the effects are palpable: in one area of the Scottish Highlands, applications for rural practices by qualified doctors dropped from more than eighty per vacancy in 1980 to one full- and one part-time applicant in 2000. Yes, one might attribute this decline of interest to a number of other factors, but talking with rural doctors in Scotland and the United States over many years has made one thing glaringly obvious to me: these people know that there are things that they do better than their institutionalized colleagues, but they are things that those colleagues will never know or indeed come to care much about. As a rural doctor-friend once put it with reference to his relationship with his local medical-school experts,

You see, the problem is that . . . I am smarter than they are, but [my colleagues] will never know that (the idea that someone in my line of work could be smart). Because the thing is every time they interact with me, they interact on their terms. For example, if I talk to a cardiologist, no matter how much I know, he knows more about cardiology than I do. If I talk to a gastroenterologist, he knows more. He doesn't realize how much I know . . . because our only interaction is on his terms. And, so, from the point of view of doctoring, he doesn't see me as a smart person. And he may recognize at some point that there's a lot that I do that he can't do; but there's no way he could realize how much you have to know to do a good job at what I do.[2]

And what are the things these doctors know? Of the forms of knowledge in which they excel, the most important by far concerns their understanding of what it means to be an "outsider"; for the perceived communal need for a GP is less frequently the outcome of villagers seeing the doctor as "one of them" than as someone who, for whatever reason, has chosen to live among those who themselves feel neglected by the cultural mainstream (Williams 1998). In other words, the doctor's experience of the world beyond that local community is more important than his being "one of us"; for the doctor's strength derives directly from being betwixt and between worlds—a liminal transformer, a guide to the sick, who may not only live a bit on the edge of things, but sometimes be recognized as an outright eccentric (Berger 1967). This explains why many of the best rural physicians I have met are, despite what some studies have indicated (Rabinowitz et al. 2001), urban transplants; for an advocate who is between two worlds is in the long run much more crucial to the survival and resilience of a rural community than is the local kid whose horizons are set, if he or she gets good enough, somewhere at or near the big city. The doctor who grew up on the farm, or in the mining town, or in the local trailer park is much more valuable to a university that can "showcase" her than she is to the local community that may live in suspicion of her loyalties.

To succeed where the lights are less bright, a doctor must make good use of the "exotic" opportunities provided, on the one hand, by the big world of corporate medicine and, on the other, by the strange—yes, now exotic—world of provincial meaning. Because a good doctor is primarily a "facilitator," doctors are most successful when they walk the line between their patients' needs and the social and governmental institutions that control access to the resources on which a patient's health depends. Her successes are (as they always have been) measured by an ability to be both a sponsor for, and an advocate of, the patients among whom she lives and works.

Successful doctors always walk this line, and it is surprising in the extreme that medical centers should believe themselves to be advancing primary care by trying to control the social space in which primary-care identity is defined. To give rural doctors Internet access, for example, as a way of attending to rural health-care needs is, at least at the level of human meaning, not only to have missed what is really important to their successful survival in the bush, but to have expanded institutional power yet more deeper into those "uncultivated" lands. Why should anyone wonder then why so many of those computers remain unused by the physicians whose lives were meant to have been profoundly bettered by learning the "truth" form some expert in London or New York? Indeed, why should anyone be at all surprised when the presence of a visiting primary-care "specialist" from a far-off medical school is greeted at the rural clinic with ambivalence, if not cynicism? When what patients ask for are advocates, further evidence of the long arm of "big brother" does little to induce trust. In this respect, the rural doctor is no different than the anthropologist who teaches "outside the Ivy," except that the liminal anthropologist's colleagues at important universities have perhaps more thoroughly co-opted the cloak of liminal advocacy.

*   *   *

So, in concluding this brief examination of the effects of contemporary institutional life on our capacities to grow and change, permit me to outline the shape of my argument concerning the entropic effects of extending, at times indefinitely, our transformational encounters with the exotic. At the risk of oversimplifying, this summary can be offered in as few as nine statements:

1) What we are observing in the examples I have provided in this brief study are processes of human psychological change—not the kind of psychological self-reflection characteristic of depth psychology, which tries to promote unself-conscious embodiment through overly self-conscious reflection, but the kind of change witnessed worldwide in rites of transformation.

2) While modern "pseudo-rites of passage," if you will, parallel the structure of traditional rites—the initial destabilization, the liminality, the reassimilation of some new identity into the everyday world—they differ in significant ways. Unlike a collective rite, which takes place in a particular group (or age set) over a determined period of time, the forms of contemporary change we have described as being extended, if not deregulated, have quite variable durations and hence equally individualized outcomes.

3) Because the liminality that signals change may be extended indefinitely, transformation can only be known retrospectively. If, that is, a rite may last a lifetime, we can excuse taking risks indefinitely because we can always claim to be extending our liminal experiences in anticipation of resolving them yet more comprehensively. In the absence of the collectively organized marking—literally "normalizing," that is, "measuring"—of time, the necessary encounter with risk that is the catalyst for change often seems far too dangerous—read, "wrong"—to us.

4) Because the catalytic function of this risk becomes forgotten over time, we regularize it as stress—that is, we subvert that uncertainty by naming its logos. In short, we "pathologize" it.

5) Our unwillingness to engage risk has then the effect of our possibly changing less while our hysterical fear of change induces the feeling that we are surely changing more.

6) An attempt to rectify the problem is evidenced in our eventually engaging in the therapeutic "writing of passage"—the ad nauseam whining about how we and others "feel."

7) This inscribing takes place in the absence of the visceral awareness of the mutating of one's identity that would have been central to the psychophysical realities of a formal rite, the mutating that would have obviated the need to write in the first place.

8) Like any other passage rite, one can no more go back to an earlier unenlightened moment than one can deliberately become unself-conscious

about having been transformed. Nostalgia, as Lasch (1991:82–119) rightly observed, encourages us not only to look back, but not to move at all. It especially prohibits us from looking forward, because it replaces transformation with sentimentality, thereby inducing the immobilization—and stagnation—of identity.

9) Responses to our being so emotionally removed from the catalyst are witnessed in the ways in which modern institutions attempt to control our need for change—even while they themselves are so incapable of changing—and in the degree to which we defer our encounters with our own emotional needs.

It is this final claim to which the conclusion of this book will be devoted.

Transnational House

> *"Is this Kansas City, Kansas, or Kansas City, Missouri?"*
>
> —*W. C. Fields*, International House

Some minutes into W. C. Fields's once-controversial "International House," the actor is shown sitting in his "autogiro," a helicopter-like contraption, the purpose of which is to take him on an epic world tour. As he travels randomly around the globe, he makes headlines by tossing empty beer bottles from his flying machine in what already in 1933 could be described as a postmodern commentary on the epic journey. The film, much controlled by Fields's eclectic interests, was long banned because of its suggestive humor and its exploration, even at this early date, of the effects of marijuana on perception. The late Cab Calloway, black lawyer and jazz musician, gesticulates wildly as he sings "have you ever seen that funny reefer man?" in a scene that kept the full version of the film out of theaters for decades.

Like the radioscope itself—the early television whose Chinese inventor in the movie provides the foil for Fields's absurd humor—the film is driven, if this is the right word, by an inability to synchronize images with voice-over or with time itself. Space, similarly, is represented as highly malleable; for Fields's journey takes him accidentally to Wu-Hu, China, after he purportedly removes the needle from his compass to darn a pair of socks. When his plane comes to a crashing halt in the middle of dinner at a hotel's roof-garden restaurant, he yells from the flying machine to the first person he sees: "Hey, Charlie . . . where am I?" "This is the roof garden of the International Hotel," replies the hotel manager. Then Fields sets off:

FIELDS: Never mind the details. What town is it?
MANAGER: This is Wu-Hu, China.

FIELDS: Then what am I doing here?
MANAGER: Well, how should I know?
FIELDS: Well, what is Wu-Hu doing where Kansas City oughta be?
MANAGER: Maybe you're lost . . .
FIELDS: Kansas City is lost. I am here!

Were the film contemporary, it may well have been called "Transnational House," for it parodies virtually all of the ironies of postmodernity that strike us today as novel and unique—except that it did so nearly seventy years ago. At one point, Fields even enacts what must be the first-known example of the modern bumper-sticker command to "Kill Your Television." As its Chinese inventor attempts to align images with voice-over for the many international guests who have flocked to the hotel to buy the rights to the then-new invention, Fields suddenly appears dressed in a silk robe, smoking a hookah, and wearing his top hat (of course). When the images of battleships appear on the radioscope's screen, he withdraws his pistol, shoots, and sinks one of the ships. Actors talk from within the television to outsiders acting in the movie and even respond to them as fellow participants in various encounters that can only be called surreal.

Though no written description could do justice to this bizarre film—especially in today's filmic vocabulary, where, in order to be marketable, movies must be pitched as commercial pabulum to a twelve-year-old mind—its overall effect is prophetic, even if, or perhaps especially because, its humor might today be lost on so many of us, including, or perhaps especially, on those purveyors of what passes for high thinking in Hollywood. Everything, at least on the surface, appears to be characterized by disjunction, chaos, and speed—all of which are embedded in the race to purchase the rights to the new imaging invention.

Fields, delightfully oblivious of all of the "important" people who have come to the hotel, eventually finds himself the object of the financially motivated affections of Peggy Hopkins Joyce, the wealthy Hollywood actress who plays herself in the film. And it is his ignorance and disregard for all of the inflated people he parodies, along with their vapid corporate institutions, that ultimately makes this film much more than postmodern, because his ignoring those very institutional and corporate powers—buffooning as he does the superficial rubbish that passed for importance in his day and yet still does in ours—is also his ticket to transcendence. Let me explain.

OF MAUSS AND CORPORATE MEN

"We interrupt this program to bring you a special announcement."

Ever since 1886, when corporations in the United States succeeded in legislating themselves into personhood,[3] their ambiguous identities have allowed them the privileges of individuals without the moral obligations that have always been an expected—if idealized—part of being human. Though corporations may sometimes be incited to give philanthropically, they do not, and cannot, possess empathic capacities. Their "personhood" is in fact a legal convenience that entitles them as would-be people to spend as much as they like on propaganda—that is, to advertise and say what they will—because limiting their spending would limit their right to express themselves and, therefore, infringe upon their personal right to free speech. This means, essentially, that all of the important people who run them—and in the film vie for ownership of the radioscope—also have no moral obligation when it comes to the activities of this corporate "person." In fact, this is exactly what limited liability (Ltd.) means, and why the CEOs of so many businesses that go bottom up are not personally liable for company errors unless they themselves have behaved illegally. In the film, the race to China rings prophetically as a premonition of contemporary free-trade excess.

Corporations are, in other words, by definition gutless, entirely nonvisceral "people." They are so thoroughly incapable of empathy that they are less *immoral* than *amoral.* They are neither good nor bad "people," but only pragmatic and self-interested "people," which is why America's primary response to religious fundamentalism, both at home and abroad, is less a moral response than an economic one: go and spend more money; show your faith in America's abilities to trade and consume. Because they lack empathy, these "people" also lack the ability to reciprocate empathically, which is why they will always seek to grow in size and to do whatever is necessary to maintain their autonomy and to increase their market shares without concern for the losses of others, and why they must use their rights to free speech to remind us through commercial advertising on so-called "public" radio of their charitable nature. Capitalism is, remember, by definition no more or less than the act of using money to make more money.

However, though corporations—these "incorporated" accumulators of capital—will grow whenever possible, this apparent strength is also their very weakness; for when they do eventually bring themselves down, they have no way of gauging the morality of what they do. Though big businesses may be run by real, if emotionally "virtual," people, these "people" will always take whatever they can and do so whenever opportunities arise, because the value of anything is determined solely by what a seller of a commodity manages to extort from a buyer. Enough, that is, is never enough because wildly fluctuating values destabilize currencies and make trade difficult.

This need for predictability—that is, the need to know what a buyer will pay or can be made to pay—is, in a nutshell, why the CEOs of big business cannot escape "life in the slow lane," because they are, by constitution, allergic to variability; they thrive on unilineal growth. In other words, the overwhelming need to keep the corporate ship afloat renders these "chiefs" progressively impotent when it comes to the real task of being creative, for creativity by definition is a very risky enterprise. This is why so many of today's businessmen actually display a deep cynicism by which they sympathize with, and at times even make heroes of, those among their ranks who get caught red-handed in one dirty deal or another; for their businesses, as legal "people," lack by definition the capacity for the very forms of social action on which reciprocal moral behavior depends. This is also why corporations—as legal "people"— express no guilt over not paying taxes, because a tax is a contribution to some communal good. Businesses, especially big ones, are in this sense without spirit or soul (Marchand 1998); they are not, that is to say, *animated*.

How important is this acceptance of a corporation's essential amorality to an understanding of why we seem so resistant to real change in our new global village? Here is a typical example of recognizing its importance offered not by a university Marxist, but by a sports writer for my local small-town newspaper. This example is, in other words, deliberately chosen to illustrate that being capable of perceiving the soulless spirit of a corporation is not limited to meditating academics. Describing the late-night commercialization of baseball, he asks who in their right mind would want to let a child stay up these days to watch our national sport of baseball—the sport, remember, to which politicians regularly flock as a gesture of solidarity with the American people—or their local sponsors. But in this all-American game money talks, for

the networks want to show the games as late as possible to get prime time viewership. Prime time viewers justify the ad rates. Ad revenue funds TV's rights fees to owners. The owners then pay the players. What is missing in the equation? The fans. . . .

And now money is giving parents another issue. Ad sales drive the whole economic engine of sports, of course, and that engine isn't too fussy about its fuel as long as it's green.

Even this year's later-afternoon [Little] League Championship Series games had commercials that charitably can be called unsuitable for children, unless you call screaming prostitutes and close-ups of bloody knives family-friendly.

Those were the ads for the new Jack the Ripper flick, catchily titled "From Hell." My children are 9- and 5-year old girls, thank you very much. Does my family need this at 4 p.m.? Why on earth would anyone green-light those ads at that hour?

Oh, sorry, I forgot. Greed.

It didn't get much better during the World Series, except that most of the action was after my kids' bedtime.

But we had ads for all those charming FOX shows, the suggestive ones like "Temptation Island 2" and the scary ones like "24" and "X Files." One friend said he didn't have to tune out some commercials with the remote because his kids were frightened enough to do it themselves. . . .

I am by no means advocating censorship or seeking to bridge First Amendment right, here.[4] Rather, Major League Baseball needs to think about its moral obligations and do the right thing.

Toning down those ads may even make financial sense in the long run. After all, baseball's future is dependent on its continuing to attract young fans.

If kids can't watch, how can they become fans? (Kirkaldy 2001:1B)

Notice that this outraged columnist does not—and quite rightly—say that businesses have this responsibility, because we all know that they do not and, even though they are "people," cannot have such a responsibility—unless they, as he surmises, perceive the wearing of a new morality as financially strategic. If, that is, they do not have the priority of accruing as much money as possible, they can be sued by their shareholders for negligence.

This tendency is perhaps nowhere so clearly seen as in the media's marketing strategies. The above example—where young children are helplessly subjected to graphic images of multiply stabbed corpses while watching a game of football—provides one end of the marketing scam. However, though less sensational, the manipulation of the elderly by the media demonstrates even more convincingly that the clothes of the corporate emperor have no moral fabric. In a recent study of media stereotypes and aging, for instance, Donlon, Ashman, and Levy (2003) discovered that aging TV viewers were less concerned with whether they were negatively or positively stereotyped by the media than they were troubled by the fact that the stereotypes presented were unrealistic. Watching television, it turns out, increases the elderly viewer's sense of loneliness, which leads in turn to significantly decreased levels of self-esteem among those elderly who watch television more; for the absence of images of what is feasible results in a diminished sense that positive growth—that is, personal transformation—is feasible.

Well, one might argue, if one wanted to solve this problem, all one need do is create media images of the elderly that more accurately reflect the actual experiences of an increasingly aging population. But here is where the problem certainly becomes more mischievous, if not more interesting: for again we find that television is driven by amoral capital: in fact, the elderly are deemed basically irrelevant to the "money-vision" market for consumer goods because they do not spend enough. They are so irrelevant, in fact, that people over 65 years of age are primarily stereotyped in television commercials as consumers of medicines for their failing bodies. There is elderly money in drugs but not Disneyworld. So corporate TV employs the stereotypes of the elderly that conform to the prejudices about the aging of *younger* viewers who have money to spend.

Thus understood, television can now be proven by some future study to be a quantifiable risk factor among the elderly. But even now such a startling conclusion may be readily corroborated in the reporting by the elderly that the most unrealistic and irrelevant representations of the aging occur first on commercial TV, followed more distantly by cable TV, where programs are paid for by subscription. Asked why he thought that the most acceptable stereotypes of the elderly occurred on British television, one viewer answered without hesitation: "it's because the programs are not driven by commercial sponsors." The free capital market in television, in other words, may be understood as a direct threat to well-being. Here the detachment of the elderly becomes but one part of that haunting emotional disjunction of Mander's TV viewers, which in turn is but a part of that cultural disembodiment wherein what we claim to believe has little or nothing in common with what we do.

So, like reforming campaign lobbyists, finding a strategy for solving the problem is part of the problem, except that now it is not only a matter of restricting campaign funding which cannot happen without the approval of those who are handsomely funded, but also of reversing the "personhood" of the corporation enough to restrict what kids must endure in order for this business "person" to flourish. Are there limits to what we should then allow of technology and free capital, if the corporation is but an amoral person? Censorship and restricting free speech are unconstitutional even if we must now face the fact that new forms of genocide have been directly attributed to the expression of free speech through the media (Mironko forthcoming).

In other words, it is *the job* of corporations to prey with precision upon the misfortunes of others while claiming to work in the public interest. Any photo of a child laborer in the era of Carnegie or Rockefeller—or, if you could get it, any photo-essay on a Third-World sweatshop—will graphically make this point. Decades ago, when my mother's grandfather had his arm torn off in a mill accident, he was taped up and sent home for good—to beg, borrow, or steal some sustenance for his now used-up body. Even today, workman's compensation should not be mistaken for corporate goodwill; it exists because workers demanded it. It is easy, both morally and financially, for corporations to behave philanthropically once they have destroyed the competition: "just give me everything and I will make good use of it."[5] It is fairly easy to downgrade one's own paranoia about not succeeding once we have taken as much as we possibly can. Though some may wish after the fact to idealize the charity of our robber barons, even the most politically conservative of us recognize the fact that there is no column for morality in corporate accounting. As Shattuck reminds us in his challenging study of the limits of freedom, "The knowledge that our many sciences discover is not forbidden in and of itself. But the human agents who pursue that knowledge have never been able to stand apart from or control or prevent its application to our lives" (1996, 225). One could, of course, cite some very impressive research to make an argument about the amoral social impact of corporate practice,[6] but I raise the local sports example because I merely wish the reader to evidence *how common it now is today to accept the inevitable amorality of having the option of both being and not being a person.*

Partially this advantage is a matter of convenience—purchase your neatly vested friend in court—a.k.a. "democratically elected" representative—and you can basically behave as you like; but at the level of reciprocity, the problem of both being and not being a person—that is, of being a *monster*—is much more complex, because the "body" of the corporation is not made up of feelings, but of assets. These assets include both its financial and material assets and its work force, which must be sufficiently integrated so that the activities of various members are appropriate for whichever domain of the corporate body each individually inhabits. Exceptional catalytic activities on the part of any single institutional member who occupies only a small part of that body are, by analogy, much like a growing tumor. And no one, at least as far as I know, has ever examined the psychological consequences for human growth of exchanging personal awareness for a bit part in the corporate monster's cannibal feast.

This built-in amorality itself explains why corporations promote conformity by coaxing everyone at a given level of prestige to behave similarly—why employee achievements are measured more by their ability to conform than by their enthusiasm for creative growth. The free-market argument—that deregulating the flow of capital yet further induces healthy competition—is, in other words, only a ruse for allowing corporate institutions to suppress the very autonomy and independence that they supposedly embrace. There is, and can be, no freedom to engage in reciprocal exchange—to participate in a moral economy—as long as it remains impossible to step behind the smoke screen of the corporate monster and deal directly with the guy who calls himself, and is called by his employees, The Wizard of Oz. Big businesses, big governments, and big universities are identical then, at least insofar as their very institutional stability is what makes them increasingly complacent.

Despite all of the rhetoric about corporate innovation, in other words, the bottom line is that every CEO is protecting a coat of arms, a lifestyle. Good ideas are mildly interesting as long as they do not infringe upon the cocktail hour, the yacht on order, or the grotesque stock option. When our Mr. Greenspan speaks out in surprise at our collective absence of corporate trust, he is not only, as his surname might otherwise indicate, talking about how to stretch a dollar; for complacency at a distance is a dangerous thing: read Richard Rhodes on the moral tribulations of Hitler's murderers (2002) and you will see precisely the deindividualizing outcomes of "corporate" passivity in their starkest formulation. Nazis, in this sense, are people for whom nothing is worth the abandoning of the status quo. They are, as it were, totally "incorporated" people.

Now, you may say, "my colleagues could never engage in such brutality." I say, judging from their retirement portfolios, "just wait"; for the majority of my colleagues, and virtually *all* of their green investment advisors, have never made an unannounced visit to one of those foreign sweatshops where laundered goods are churned out for our home-based champions of free trade. In what way, to put it bluntly, is that Asian factory any different than the mill that harvested my great grandfather's arm? It makes no difference to the corporate monster whether that cheap microwave is made by a person, by a machine, or by a monkey as long as the institution—academic, governmental, or business—keeps itself "healthy."

Believe it or not, smart people still remain mystified as to why globalization has not produced the essential betterment of the majority of the world's citizens who live on less than one dollar a day. The answer is that any country with great need is vulnerable to the hope that the future is a better place; but it is equally vulnerable to not recognizing how the corporation-as-person must, until it has conquered all competitors, remain indifferent to the misery of the poor. This is why those corporations will eventually leave Taiwan and Calcutta just as they left Baltimore and Pittsburgh. This is why colleges and universities continuously manicure their lawns and buildings while their classrooms are feverishly remodeled to accommodate yet one more feature film about the latest famine in East Africa. Though their nonprofit status might render them less obviously amoral, their need for institutional conformity leaves them wholly vulnerable to their own passionless self-interest.

And it is this need for institutional conformity that in the end makes diversity impossible; because diversity can no more be enforced than can an attraction to the so-called "exotic." How then can we expect an awareness of diversity among our children, or students, or colleagues at work, if we cannot accept that something alien or exotic might redefine who we are or what we do? How can we demand diversity of others if we ourselves are incapable of either recognizing or accommodating it?

"Les techniques du corporations"; or, Life in the Slow Lane

> *Equally innocent and infinite are the pleasures of observation and the resources engendered by the habit of analyzing life.*
>
> —*Henry James, "The Middle Years"*

So why pick on wealthy, self-interested money mongers? After all, aren't those of us who work for academic corporations equally culpable? Don't we all participate in the selfsame moral ruse every time part of our paycheck gets invested in a retirement fund that is tied to the stock market? Why pick on the poor rich kids when at least they are honest about their motivations? Are academic and nonprofit corporate "bodies" any freer when it comes down to the amorality of making money on the backs of the less fortunate, or are they actually worse for being less open about their financial motivations than those crass businesspeople they both imitate and criticize?

Are academic corporations, in other words, any less prone to corporate behavior than the businesses they, on one level, look down upon and, on another, desire as bedfellows? At the time when I came up for my professorial tenure review, to cite a personal example, I remember being informed that the diversity of my professional interests left administrators wondering about my institutional loyalty. As a relatively young academic, the criticism seemed unfair, especially since at that very moment *every* head administrator of my college had job applications pending elsewhere. What I had yet, of course, to appreciate was the degree to which the smooth functioning of corporations requires that they discourage any professional enthusiasm that might be construed as disproportionate to the activities of other employees who occupy similar positions within the institutional hierarchy. (In my case, it was even suggested that I relax and take up golf!)

Ideologically, of course, all of this makes perfect sense, because if you cannot make discriminations, your only real option is to regulate—that is, to define another's performance by some common standard—by getting everyone basically *to do the same thing*. Corporations—on Wall Street and in Cambridge— are not at all unlike uncovered grain silos standing out in an open farm field. At their bottom levels, the grain is packed tightly—in fact, so tightly that it ferments and intoxicates—while on the open top, the lighter grain can easily be swept away into the top of another nearby silo.

It was, in other words, entirely appropriate for my administrators to be talking about institutional loyalty at the same time as they were each seeking employment elsewhere. All corporations, like all grain silos, stand or fall on their ability to produce enough fermentation at their bases to stupefy the drones who fill them. On the level of such intoxication then, nonprofits and charitable organizations are somewhere off the charts. Because employees are, generally speaking, not well situated to enhance the corporate coffers, they lack the competitive spirit that drives capitalism (unless, of course, they are in scientific fields that produce significant slush funds for their institutions through indirect costs on awarded grants[7]) while wanting at the same time to demonstrate that they are somehow better (read, "more committed to the institution") than the person in the next cubicle.

The result unsurprisingly is that stasis is encouraged, even in the name of discovery, if not in that of fairness. Stasis, in fact, is such a measure of success that there is little or no mobility, as the literature on nongovernmental organizations (NGOs) clearly shows,[8] from one silo to the next at the lower levels. The intoxication of loyalty—of the measurement of one's institutional contribution—is held over one's head much like the pressure produced at the bottom of the silo by the tons of grain stored above. This is why silos are wrapped in steel bands—because the pressure from above is so great that they would burst were they constructed in the manner of any other kind of holding tank. They are, in other words, immobilizing structures whose very design inhibits growth.

Like then the phallic silo that the modern corporation resembles, each institution will have at its head someone whose success is predicated on not only an ability to remain mobile, but on his or her ability to move with the wind—which, of course, is why sailing is the preferred domain in which corporate excess gets expressed. CEOs survive, in large measure, not by invention or intellectual skill, but by positioning themselves vaguely enough never to be pigeonholed. At the same time, they reward themselves handsomely—for many corporations from fifty times to as much as five hundred times the wages they pay their average drones.[9] This unequal distribution of wealth means that CEOs depend upon lateral mobility—because they have no more vertical mobility within their organization—even though they are almost entirely unknown outside of the silo in which they have unchallenged status, or outside of those adjacent silos where they may seek yet better rewards. If you are the president of a college or university, for instance, people will address you by your title, even though there are more than 2,000 of you in America alone, and repeated challenges to my students to name a single president of a college other than their own virtually always results in complete silence. In the popular view, Bill Gates—whose name is not queried by my computer's spell-checker—is the national hero who funds well-intentioned academics and charities; it gets pretty thin after that.

This is why such presidents are all eventually encouraged by their boards of trustees to seek employment elsewhere—even while those trustees have undermined the very notion of a liberal arts institution by settling permanently on the borders of the institutions they are meant only to oversee. Forget the potential for conflicts of interest on the part of these overseers and the fact that their often poor behavior goes largely unanalyzed, because the principal test of the wisdom of the initial appointment of a CEO—a.k.a. the "president"—comes only much later on when another similar organization ratifies your choice by trying to hire him. Those overseers must facilitate this because the worst thing you can do is overstay your visit by appearing permanent, or even more troubling, by setting up a local shop after your reign has ended. Anyone familiar with how dowry functions in India to feign upward mobility will understand this troubling condition of advancement exactly. "Marrying up," in other words, is not only a technique by which connubial achievers improve their status. The corporate emperor is no exception to this tendency.

One might, however, reasonably ask why under such conditions of anonymity CEOs are permitted by shareholders to reward themselves in such undignified ways; for even the best performers cannot fully justify the excessive level of remuneration so often witnessed. To understand this apparently illogical tendency, one must remember that it is where social identity is most contested—read "insecure"—that the need to distinguish that leader in financial terms is greatest. Under insecure conditions basically everyone actually wants this because patrician sentiment—the sort of idea whereby you become thankful enough for your own fortune that you feel the need to plow your shares into some common coffer of goodness—is wholly unknown among the upward and aggressively mobile. Is it any wonder that Sennett (1998) should lament the absence of CEOs on community and hospital boards—that is, that they should be so disinclined today to involve themselves on the whole in local goodwill? For such upward mobility is the exact antithesis of what Buddhists and Hindus call "dharma"—that is, of achievement measured as the outcome of some socially integrated sense of self-purpose. In this regard, CEOs are the exact opposite of our aforementioned rural doctors who more or less define a small community and who in turn define themselves at the level of the community they both represent and serve.

But in settings of extreme upward mobility—in the world of the CEO or the grant-driven academic—the only measure of success becomes more and more *excess*. Though American CEOs can, as mentioned, make as much as five hundred times the salary of the average laborer, they on average still accrue on the order of eighty-five times the salary of the corporate wage earner, while in Europe—where one's status is, generally speaking, less achieved—that ratio is far less. And in Japan, where openly stuffing one's fist in the collective jar is considered unmannerly, that ratio drops from eighty-five to less than twenty times the salary of the woman on the shop floor. Here one must remind oneself of just how tied is our social ignorance to our having given over to big business that which defines a person. Indeed, as we increasingly distance ourselves from genuine forms of transformation in social space, we actually encourage this inequality, vapid though the personalities of "leaders" may be; for we now more than ever need what we think can be cheaply achieved by manufacturing increasingly petty forms of status in the workplace. In the absence of an embodied sense of what risk can bring, in other words, almost any imitative form will do, thank you very much.

And what of the "head" of the corporate body? Like the NGO director who moves from UNICEF to CARE to WHO, these heads of what we yet unabashedly call academic institutions may be as empty as that grain silo after a long winter, but the commonality of the institutions they manage allows them to pass for moral beings across those domains because paradoxically they have preserved an appearance of conformity that transcends what they may or may not know or feel morally. Indeed, once their Goffman-like "passing" is unveiled, one readily sees how the more they build their nonprofit institutions into businesses, the less possible it becomes for them to define their behavior—for reasons already mentioned—in moral terms.

Setting aside the details of such minor ambition, the important point is that the increasing absence of collective moral rites within the modern life we all must accept persuades even the most cautious of us to see these corporations as supplements for our undiminished religious needs. Attend a gathering of alumni at any American college or university and you will find that you may well still experience behaviors that can make even a seasoned socialite blush.

For increasingly, it seems, our "passing" is not at all unlike that described for the poorest parts of the world—as in Zaire, for instance, where individuals may bluff their way into the best jobs even though they have no qualifications. Here people, in the words of philosopher Jean Luc Aka-Evy, "wear what they have so everyone knows they have something" (Hecht and Simone 1994:48); here "designer clothes can be profitably resold or repeatedly rented-out"; here some tailors even create successful fantasies of what Africans hoped that Westerners had marketed, despite the fact that everyone knows they are fakes.

Curious though these "foreign" practices may appear to those not engaged in them, it is hard to see such descriptions as at all unlike the degradations of contemporary academic life. It was for similar reasons, by the way, that Marilyn Monroe identified her favorite fantasy—namely, the removing of her clothes before a church congregation. For the Hollywood star, the erotic thrill of not wearing anything at all would have made it possible for everyone to see that indeed she did have something, as opposed to the institutional "emperor"—president or priest—whose nakedness is masked rather more subtly by gray or black wool. Replace "symbols of diversity" for "designer clothes" and you may find yourself courted as the next leader of one or another of our great academies.

But these are not original insights. They are obvious to all of us if we allow ourselves a mere moment to consider them. So, why then should we feel troubled by the current laughable conditions of the life of the mind? Why, moreover, should any of this strike us as odd? First it is odd that we should be so unwilling to consider the deep implications of eliminating basic forms of reciprocity when we allow for the legal formation of the corporation-as-person. Second, and probably more troubling, is the fact that we should become so accustomed to the absence of real people in these environments of "incorporation." Though we all intuitively sense why big corporations push compliant idiots into political office, why can't we fathom the reasons for a public's loss of confidence in the "economy" every time one such puppet gets, as we say, "elected" by a minority of eligible voters? Why do we seem surprised when we are betrayed by corporations that now bear no responsibility to reinvest their capital in any nation, any state, or among any other collectivity of real people?[10] Is there any good reason why such behaviors should strike us as either unfair or unexpected? Yes, if we cling to the false belief that the corporation-as-person is capable of human emotion, that it has a soul. No, if we accept the fact that this monster of a person can never be capable of that empathy on which all genuine forms of human reciprocity are based. Thus considered, the word "antitrust" might today be invested with an entirely new and unexpected meaning.

So, passively at least, we all know that the corporation-as-person is now and forever shall be amoral. And though we, on paper anyway, still have the ability to legislate away the rights that corporations have to being legal people, in reality these democratic rights become increasingly absent as we ourselves un-learn the pleasures of risking change. Yes, do vote them out; but first you have to galvanize depressed voters. Good luck.

Though the present revival of public interest in national causes might dis-courage us from seeing ourselves as others see us, it must surely be worth at-tempting if doing so allows us to see why, despite our better judgments, we sometimes elevate those whose political manners could only be characterized as ludicrous. As one pundit put it in an anonymous Internet parody attributed to a politician from Zimbabwe:

Imagine that we read of an election occurring anywhere in the third world in which the self-declared winner was the son of the former prime minister and that former prime minister was himself the former head of that nation's secret police (CIA).

Imagine that the self-declared winner lost the popular vote but won based on some old colonial holdover (Electoral College) from the nation's pre-democracy past. Imag-ine that the self-declared winner's "victory" turned on disputed votes cast in a province governed by his brother.

Imagine that the first cousin of the self-declared winner worked for a foreign owned media outlet, and that media outlet declared—prematurely and incorrectly—that the self-declared winner (the former prime minister's son) was the new president.

Imagine that the poorly drafted ballots of one district, a district heavily favoring the self-declared winner's opponent, led thousands of voters to vote for the wrong candi-date. Imagine that members of that nation's lowest caste, concerned for their fu-tures/livelihoods, turned out in record numbers to vote in opposition to the self-declared winner's candidacy.

Imagine that state police, operating under the authority of the self-declared winner's brother, intercepted numerous members of that lowest caste on their way to the polls.

Imagine that six million people voted in the disputed province and that the self-declared winner's "lead" was only 500+ votes—fewer, certainly, than the vote counting machines' margin of error.

Imagine that the self-declared winner and his political party opposed a more careful by-hand inspection and re-counting of the ballots in the disputed province or in its most hotly disputed district.

Imagine that the self-declared winner, himself a governor of a major province, had the worst human rights record of any province in his nation and actually led the nation in executions.

Imagine that a major campaign promise of the self-declared winner was to appoint like-minded human rights violators to lifetime positions on the high court of that nation.

Imagine that the advisors to the self-declared winner counseled the legislators in the province ruled by the self-declared winner's brother that they should ignore the edict of the highest court in the province regarding election laws, and that they should seize the initiative to declare the self-declared winner the winner, regardless of the judicial process or rule of law.

None of us would deem such an election to be representative of anything other than the self-declared winner's will-to-power. All of us, I imagine, would wearily turn the page thinking that it was another sad tale of pitiful pre- or antidemocracy peoples in some strange elsewhere.

Despite one's political sympathies, the absence of any real resistance to such occurrences allows us to recognize just why so few gifted young people have any interest whatsoever in pursuing a life in corporate government while at the same time, those very individuals seem capable of remaining alarmingly passive about how politicians actually behave.

Asked then what the relevance might be of institutional survival strategies in a discussion of human transformations, and our response is now obvious: *corporations are positioned not only to discourage any of us from succeeding in our individual initiatives, but to encourage passivity—even pretending in a transparently superficial manner to fulfill our deep hunger for religion.*

The veracity of this view may be evidenced not only in the ways in which individual initiative is discouraged within both corporations and within life in general, but in the actual behaviors that corporations reward. Indeed, in the absence of environments of transformation, we must of necessity satisfy ourselves with something less than human. For whatever may constitute our "travels in amodernity," we can be assured that they will involve the risk-minimizing strategy of "running in place"—of getting everyone to do the same sorts of things, because the emperor—having lost his clothes long ago—now has lots of designer supplements with which to experiment—clothes that while superficially diverse in style and color are all made of a uniform gray fabric possessing the most exquisite insulating qualities.

The tendency of academic colleges and universities to demand employee allegiance—even while their top-heavy administrators otherwise occupy themselves—reminds us of how the sublimation of sanctioned transformational rites today gets replaced by largely vapid religions of institutional loyalty. Japanese businesses are not, in other words, the only examples of such corporate bonding. Like the African imposter who offers clothes as sacrifice to fashion-conscious spirits (Hecht and Simone 1994:49–50), our alumni organizations thrive on pseudoreligious rites within which the superficial itself becomes an admirable end; for the possibility of long-lasting transformation has been all but eliminated now that the constructive potential of a rite's stress-inducing catalyst has been completely eliminated.

But why pick on academic and other nonprofit institutions in this discussion? Because of all groups of people, our intellectuals and heads of so-called charities at least ought to have the dignity to admit to us their obsessive love of corporate life as well as their knowledge that their acts of giving are, in part anyway, driven by what they may in turn force others to accept of them. In this regard, academics are no less likely to step away from the corporations they are wedded to than are the CEOs of major businesses. In fact, they may be far less likely because their supposed disinterest in the life of commerce requires that they overstate the powers of their institutions to control and bond all of us. It is far more difficult to remove oneself if one can prove that being wedded to an institution results more from its power over us than from our secret love affair with conformity. If one has not enough courage simply to move on, why not inflate the powers of the thing that controls you? All of which is to say that if we find ourselves incapable of devising some way of depersonalizing the corporate monster we have created, our "be all" shall surely be the "end all" of life as we might otherwise have known it.

Slowdown or Meltdown?

In this polemic I have been enough critical of the idea of postmodernity that I might easily be seen at risk of suggesting that there is nothing unique about the contemporary conditional of transnational living. Quite the contrary; for I do gladly acknowledge that networks of transnational authority have had profound effects on daily living, but I also vigorously maintain that those effects are not entirely as they appear. Indeed, they may be the opposite of what they appear, at least at the level of human development. The combined forces of stress management, of transformational attenuation, of therapeutic writing, and of institutional conformity clearly work together to produce a reduction— not a proliferation—of personal change in contemporary life.

This reduction is seen in any number of patterns of deferral that are today sanctioned. I do not mean here only the deferral of such visceral experiences as having children or the multiple unstated rules against public displays of affection. I also mean such things as the institutional requirement that genuine players will always be "serious"; or the promotion of the belief that corporations, academic or commercial, are too important and powerful to live without; or the widespread claim that the limiting of stress is synonymous with well-being; or the absurd notion that caution is the only appropriate response to a world that is sold to us as always chaotic. If we discourage one another from actively responding to these predilections, will we then change less? Almost certainly.

Whether in some final analysis of our era we see this slowing down as a new thesis about contemporary life, or as a condition of postmodernity itself, is far less important than is the acknowledgment of this retarding phenomenon. If postmodernity involves becoming more self-conscious about one's actions, then yes, the contemporary psychoanalysts will get us no closer to meaningful visceral awareness by talking in increasingly self-conscious terms about why we seem so incapable of happiness. If a condition of postmodernity is defined by an easy willingness to give up on change, to surrender to apathy, in a world that appears to thrive on the ephemeral, then yes, these times may, in fact, have a distinctive character that deserves some epithet. Afraid of living? Consider the alternative.

The argument—that the temporal extension of transformations causes a separation of intellect from visceral awareness—has, if correct, some important and even disturbing consequences; for in extending these transformational encounters over several years we inevitably separate the power of the emotional moment from its long-term rationalization. We take ourselves, that is, away from the embodied understanding of what might be possible and move, instead, toward a less physical awareness—the stuff of intellectual ruminating.

What may have been cathartic becomes over time the ongoing fabric of our psychological disabilities, and our hopes for creating something new get similarly transformed into what we see as "pathological manifestations"—those uncertainties that we learn to describe through the controlled rhetoric of depth psychology. If slowing down then is a process of separating embodiment from knowledge, how much have our social institutions contributed to our learning about the effects of reflection on extended—that is to say, attenuated—forms of change? In fact, they have not been terribly helpful. One might without much work even argue with some success that these very modern institutions have so homogenized the concept of living that nobody could expect them to be anything other than emotionally restricting. Our medical-school admissions committees may argue that "we can make a doctor out of anyone,"[11] but the numbers of bad choices that their admissions committees make—regularly losing medical school students to other professions even when they have as many as 100 candidates for a single place—presents us with a harder reality: if your admissions are influenced by standards of research that drive what the institution can expect to make from indirect costs on grants, you shall never appreciate, let alone enthusiastically endorse, the successful doctor's liminality. To do that means not only revising the institutional values that work directly against freedom of thought, but revising the ability of corporations to function as (monstrous) people.

"Discountability" and Transcendence

> *Oh yes, well, radical is one thing but I don't know whether the sort of people, you might say these elitist people, in the know really regarded me as a radical in the sense that it is put out. I mean the term is used to nullify, it is a term of abuse. They'll give me an honourary degree when I'm dead, as soon as I'm dead, they are waiting for me. I hear about my death quite often, that I'm dead. They'll love that. Glasgow University has never invited me to give a fucking lecture in any department in my whole life. I've been asked to give lectures in pretty well every university—at least a lecture by a society or so on—but not a single lecture in Glasgow. Well, that's my home town. Well, fuck them.*
>
> —*R. D. Laing,* Mad to Be Normal

Active Dreaming

On the morning of June 7, 2003, I had a stark dream in which I was offered a single opportunity to advance an anthropological subject of my choosing before a large audience of citizens. It was an especially interesting dream because I was aware that, while one may at times speak in front of large numbers of people, it was more than dreaming on my part to think that anyone would readily have the chance to advance an idea before a group of people not already selected on the basis of some previously shared interest—how the people who might listen to me (or, for that matter, read this book) would already be inclined toward my subject, if not toward my view of it. I was aware, in other words, that the dream had made it possible for me to have a kind of social encounter that would be rare for even the best known of us and that part of what interested me was the realization of just how rare such a truly open event might be. The subject of my address, therefore, would in some way be chosen on such grounds. And in this dream, I knew immediately that, given the circumstance, I wanted to speak about something called "the principle of discountability."

What might such a principle be? I recall being initially somewhat perplexed in the dream about the name of this principle, though I knew that in some way my talk would counter the modern-day discounting of transformation—of change, of instability, of uncertainty—by illustrating to my audience not merely the contemporary prevalence of such discounting. My job, I knew, would also be to offer some suggestion regarding the means by which this downgrading of the value of the unknown might be transcended.

The principle of discountability, then, was to be understood as the cause of our modern disengagement with personal and social change. Conversely, it could also be understood as the cause of our growing search for stasis. Since the true catalysts for transformation are—as we have seen throughout this book—nearly always discounted (because those things that truly change us will initially appear to have an effect only on a minority [statistically fewer than one third] of any randomly selected cohort), it was inevitable that the majority of any destabilized group (about 70 percent of us) would tend to discount the possibilities presented by a given transformational catalyst. Under such conditions, in other words, a new or novel transformational catalyst would always be so discounted, except when this social discounting was itself brought to consciousness and addressed—at which point the public display of this weakness would erode its paralyzing abilities. This, in itself, was why in the dream it was essential to speak publicly: because the public and conscious display of this paralysis was the necessary step in limiting its control over human freedom.

It was, then, far less important in this dream that I was given the opportunity to pontificate before lots of people than that this widespread social fear was made the subject of public discourse. It wasn't that open debate would in itself enhance growth (though indeed it may) but that bringing to light the social paralysis that inhibits human growth could defuse the very power of that paralysis to produce social apathy. What transformational catalysts, consequently, all seemed to share as a central feature was (and this was my message) their discountability—the absence of any general awareness of their importance. What needed to happen, I thought, was that we become enough aware of the problem of discountability to induce some transcendence of the fear it caused.

Was this dreamt awareness—that growth today could be so widely discounted—as important as my dormant moment would have it? Frankly, I cannot say. But perhaps I can offer some indication of why I am tempted to respond in the affirmative. To do this, I would like to conclude my polemic by situating its general argument more personally—and, in particular, by discussing what I believe to be the debilitating consequences of this so-called principle of discountability for those educational settings in which our collective moral sensibilities are meant to be cultivated. By means of such a discussion, I will less revisit Chapter 5's consideration of institutional atrophy than I will suggest how the current rules of social engagement that govern our colleges and universities actually discount—and hence directly undermine—the potential we each yet possess for moral growth. Your college, in other words, may not be the friend it presents itself as, and knowing this may make your experience of it more productive, if not totally fulfilling.

You're in the Army Now

A recent plea by my department's administrative assistant for faculty to submit their course syllabi yet again called to mind just how much life in the academy has changed over the last twenty years. Anyone of my generation will have distinct memories of entering on the first day of a given college term at least one class for which there was no syllabus at all. In the Dark Ages of the 1960s and 1970s it was quite common, as mentioned earlier (p. 62), to have a professor withhold his or her decision about course readings until the class first met as a group. In most cases, there were books already in the college bookstore; but the order in which they would be read, and the assignment of related articles, had been delayed until the instructor gained some sense of who the class participants were—what their academic needs and learning capabilities were; what the size and social composition of the class recommended; what the group dynamic might be. Yes, some other decisions on readings were delayed because the professor was out getting stoned or was using these liberties to kick back and bungle through. But, for the most part, I think, we appreciated the fact that our semester would be guided as much by social agreement as by the inscribed contract that today's syllabus has become.

Of course, it is easy in retrospect to claim that an America in the midst of an unpopular war in Vietnam—an America torn by deep political division—made the academy a far less stable place than it is today. Students interrupted their studies in order to participate in all sorts of rallies, and faculty and administrators were often as much protesting with them as they were locking the doors of their offices to keep them out. I have a distinct memory, for instance, of having my admissions interview at Oberlin College canceled (I had intended to transfer there) because the dean assigned to speak with me had been hauled in by the local police for demonstrating against the Vietnam War.

Though one could write nostalgically about such levels of moral commitment, the truth was that those moments were filled with uncertainty and immense doubt. (Can you imagine such a thing today?) The war took a terrible toll on the social fabric of life both within and outside the academy: among my friends (who were not at all atypical) were soon-to-be soldiers, expatriates, and lunatics (see p. 33). Few had the wit to become a conscientious objector; fewer still had the privilege to go to graduate or professional school as a strategy for avoiding what for most of us seemed inevitable; almost no one I knew at the time could be defined as "socially aware"—at least as the term might be understood today by the properly heeled student who knows precisely where he or she would like to be working immediately following graduation.

In fact, as president of my high school class in 1966 and 1967, I remember how surprised most of us were to learn about Vietnam. There were countless young men already dead or imprisoned there, but in truth we knew little of what was actually going on. Ask to see my high school yearbook from 1968 (as even my friends today demand when I make this argument), and you will be surprised to find—despite what your history professors may argue about the levels of public awareness then—that the war did not exist for us. Even though the country was about to come apart at its seams, the more than five hundred photos of my graduating class from that yearbook each came with an opportunity to describe (in ten words or less) what one thought one's future might hold in store. The word "Vietnam" appears . . . well . . . nowhere.

Within a year or two of that moment, however, we would all discover quite rudely that the only ones who appeared to be safe from facing the exigencies of social turmoil were the smart guys with velvet hands who got themselves into Ivy League schools; for there they could be guaranteed admission into one or another graduate program, or into a professional school that would extend their student draft exemptions indefinitely. There were, of course, also the sons of politicians—like some of our country's presidents and vice-presidents— who were spared such decisions by informal executive privilege (that is, by nepotism or plain cheating), but the common kid was pretty much thrown from a state of ignorance into one of social hell in a matter of months. You could put a date on that transforming moment; for most, it was January 1968, a few months before I would graduate from high school, and the event was the Tet Offensive.

Yet, despite the overnight reality of seeing one's friends either risking their lives or being scattered across the earth, going to college was understood by all of us—even the silver-spoon kids—as a privilege. The idea that one might buy a four-year college experience—like a coat or a new pair of shoes—never entered the minds of those I knew. It wasn't that we were totally naive (unrealistic though our expectations may have been); it was just that most of us didn't identify so deeply with any particular form of institutional living. At one of the colleges I attended, less than 30 percent of the students in my class graduated together (as compared to more than 95 percent of the students at some of today's benighted institutions). I ended up attending two colleges and one university before entering graduate school, and I knew several people whose educational experiences were similarly self-constructed. It wasn't that we gave up on learning; it was just that we were for the most part unfamiliar with the idea that undergraduate life could be a consumer-driven, hand-holding event. I don't think that what we did was better or worse than what students do today, but it certainly was different.

For starts, virtually all of the American students I knew in college had parents who had lived through an awful war. Many of our fathers said little beyond Hail Marys about the things they wished they didn't have to remember, and we children knew that we were lucky, though we may not have known just why. Like the word "Holocaust" (which, as we noted, was a descriptive term created by the children of death-camp survivors to name their parents' horror), the "antiwar movement" codified by my generation was created in part as a response to parents who would rather have put the true horrors of World War II behind them. It was in this way that the 1960s were an outcome of the 1950s. In fact, the teenage years of baby boomers were not steeped in turmoil because the postwar years had been as idyllic as most now tend to think of them. The 1960s were tumultuous because we had all grown up ducking and covering as kids in school while Mom and Dad were merrily having lots of un-protected sex in an effort to forget just how awful the 1940s had been.

The 1960s, then, did not become as chaotic as they turned out to be because the 1950s that we today associate with prosperity were psychologically peace-ful. The 1960s became disruptive because my generation was responding to what our parents would just as soon have put behind them but somehow could not forget. The silence of death-camp survivors was the most dramatic exam-ple of this desire not to remember out loud; but there were thousands of Pur-ple Hearts that remained in desks and bedroom drawers. Part of this (yet ongoing) silence was because the limits of patriotic duty were for them un-questioned; part of it was because things happen in war's violent tranforma-tional moments that no one wants to remember. Of every thousand soldiers, for instance, two would get an Expert Infantry medal. My father had one that I found in a cardboard box in our basement.

What, then, are the issues that got codified in the 1960s? Though they have many names and labels, there are in effect but two: (1) What are the moral lim-its of patriotism—that is, when is it time to say that the morals of your leaders are questionable? and (2) Why should it be acceptable to forget all of the forms of human behavior—noble or hideous—that are brought to light by war?

Because these issues remained unresolved, they guaranteed that the appar-ent tranquility of the 1950s would be the catalyst for social upheaval, for the identification and naming of that holocaust called war. Because beneath the superficial prosperity of the 1950s grumbled a deep psychological instability whose transformational nature would finally be defined during the college years of every baby boomer. Lots of books have been written about this period of American history and its antiwar movement, but it might better have been understood as my generation's attempt to use higher education as a tool for en-suring that the social catalyst of World War II—the anxious transformation the war gave way to—would settle in a positive, rather than a negative, out-come.

College, then, became a very different sort of social space for baby boomers from the totally prescribed and even regimented environments that today pass for realms of higher whatever. What I mean by this is simply that we were angry at the world, but we also felt lucky to be able to learn, even if we didn't do that very well. In fact, for most of us, who we were as people was less a func-tion of where we came from on some minutely measured social scale than it was an outcome of what we did (or tried to do) as students. To have expectations driven by the upward mobility of one's parents would have seemed odd to those I knew—and I don't think that the people around me in college were at all atypical. In those days, we may have mistaken social liberty for intellectual freedom, just as today's students mistake upward mobility (where family dinner talk is nearly always about measuring money) for social status (where who you are doesn't require a big mouth). But we at least knew that we were in the midst of a transformation and that its outcome was on our shoulders.

So what does the academic chaos of the 1960s have to do with the ornately prescribed thing that the modern educational institution has become? To understand how these two diverse academic realities are connected, one has to remove the question from the emotionally volatile comparison of generations—my parent's, mine, my children's—and place it within the framework of what has been argued in this book about learning and human growth.

Man Over-Bored

Has the nature of life in our educational institutions really changed all that much? And, if it has changed, in what important ways has it done so? While I think one can certainly argue that what happens in college today is a good bit less unpredictable than it once was, it may also be less conducive to both good and bad forms of growth—that is, less transformational.

This is a big claim, but it can be readily evidenced in the ways in which our commodifying of higher learning has made it increasingly difficult for even the most motivated of students to experience anything profoundly new. As much as my cynicism may seem unwarranted, the evidence for this view is easily gathered, though its interpretation may more readily escape us. It's that same old anthropological paradox that we took up in Chapter 3: from one perspective we argue that it takes one to know one (that one is the *best* judge of what's going on in one's own life); while from another we claim that the hardest thing to know intellectually is one's own culture (that one may be the *worst* judge of what's going on in one's own life). It's a paradox the awareness of which takes place in introductory social science courses across the country when students are asked to read about that strange tribe called the Nacirema. Some get the joke right away. But for most it's only when we view the Nacirema in Marshall McLuhan's rear-view cultural mirror (when we look back at how foolishly we once behaved as we travel forward in life) that we see in reverse lettering the word "American" shouting out at us. It's only in this retrospective view, in other words, that the peculiar habits of the tribe described in the famous article are witnessed as none other than our very own.

Was my generation any better equipped to adjust the mirror poised on the (usually dysfunctional) family car of the 1960s than are today's college students to direct the one on that Audi or Honda or Ford Expedition? In addressing this question, let's take one final look at the concrete effects of the corporate marketing of college education. I have already discussed, if briefly, the over-in-scribing of course-related materials in our syllabi—over-inscribed in that the notion of real discovery gets ruled out by the absence of any need to negotiate the uncertainty of what a learning experience might be; over-inscribed because the last thing our academic business can afford is to dissatisfy consumers whose deep pockets promote a social climate that we unabashedly describe in terms more suitable to the game of golf than to the life of the mind. Instead, what I would like to do in these final paragraphs is show how there is a very good reason to be just as concerned about what we are doing to ourselves today as we might have been back in 1969.

To accomplish this, I wish to revisit for a moment the minority of students I spoke of in Chapter 4 who were able to make immediate good use of desta-bilizing internship experiences among the homeless. You may recall that of the twenty-four students involved in the program, only seven (or just under one-third) of them reported immediately following the experience that the in-ternship had been life changing; that among the remaining seventeen, the dominant feeling was that the meaningfulness of the experience had come into sharp focus only in the final days of the internship and that, if only we could provide more structure to the experience, future interns would get more out of it.

As in the classes described earlier, these students felt uncertain about what had happened, but they also felt licensed to complain about, as it were, the syl-labus. The absence of the sort of course-coddling that they had grown accus-tomed to on campus was not only nonexistent in this environment but defiantly ignored both by the angry street people (who were as likely to tell them to "fuck off" as to lay out before them a narrative of personal tragedy and human grief) and by the hospital's doctors (who felt that one's identity meant little if it was not earned). Remember also that the growth patterns of those seventeen un-committed students in the following months and years revealed the importance of an attenuated form of transformation that was characterized initially by anxieties about not knowing how one was changing—the "I'm not sure what's going on and it's your fault" feeling. Remember, finally, that over about a five-year period, the number of students who still wanted that syllabus had dwin-dled to no more than two, and my guess is that, if you come back to the remaining holdouts in another five or ten years, you should prepare yourself to meet the forty-year-old guy who went to Wall Street after graduating from col-lege but is now taking science courses in the evenings so he can apply to med-ical school.

These are, as we will now see, revealing patterns; for the point here is not only that human transformation (that is, human psychological growth) takes place over quite variable lengths of time and that, in the world which we now inhabit, only limited numbers of people are positioned to make immediate psychological use of those destabilizing moments that are the catalysts of real growth and change. The point is that these very patterns are today ubiquitous across a wide range of experiences and that the minimal number of individuals who provide early positive feedback means that we are unlikely in any institutional setting to respond favorably to the disappointments of the majority.

Now I suspect that you are thinking (just as did I at the time of the first interviews) that the reason such experiences among the homeless took variable lengths of time to assimilate was that they were, on the greater scale of things, relatively extreme. And you probably, then, are also thinking that, under so-called normal circumstances, higher degrees of satisfaction should be expressed in the interviews that would have followed the return of students from other sorts of experiences. Maybe you are even curious enough about this evidence to go out, as I did, and look at the literature on how people deal with uncertainly—from the uncertainty of buying one or another consumer product, to the uncertainty of what to do when you get deeply lost in the wilderness.

Well, if you are at all curious, I invite you to do just that. I invite you wholeheartedly to have the same learning experience that I did. Because you know what? You'll find out the same interesting thing that I did, namely that the percentage of people who do well in coping with the disappointments of not following the syllabus, or of having their brand new TV break unexpectedly, and the percentage of those who do well when lost in the woods are *exactly the same—that is, a little less than one-third*. Moreover, you'll be surprised to discover that the person who doesn't flip out when he walks four days in the wrong direction in the Canadian Rockies is statistically less often the confident graduate of NOLS, or Outward Bound, or the rock-climbing president of your college's mountaineering club who runs his siren through town as a member of the volunteer ambulance association—you know, the guy who is determined to become a graduate of the Harvard Medical School with an expertise in high-altitude pulmonary edema.

Believe it or not, the person who does well in dealing with the uncertainty of being lost or of being a political hostage is the same person who does well with a new and unfamiliar food group or who can manage when the delivery truck from the local mall brings the wrong sofa. It's this person—the one who knows how to assimilate and even at times to enjoy the uncertain experiences that living facilitates—who will do well in changing and challenging circumstance. And the percentages of such individuals among us are always just less than a third, regardless of the level of the challenge whose effects we are examining. This is, of course, not to say that a third of us will immediately do whatever is offered us as a challenge, but that a third or a bit fewer (about 30 percent on average) of any cohort will attempt to respond creatively to a destabilizing catalyst.

Interestingly, this percentage remains unaltered even in controlled settings where the presence of something transformational is merely perceived. You might, for instance, be as surprised as I was to learn that these figures also apply to the standard placebo response rate—that is, to the percentage of people who time and again experience a positive response when given a colored tablet in place of medicine, whether the tablet is an antibiotic or a form of pain medication (Moerman 2002). And what might this mean? It means that, regardless of the stimulus, about 30 percent, or just under one-third, of us will make the most out of a very unclear situation immediately following the introduction of some ambiguous variable. One therefore wonders whether the knowledge that one is participating in a placebo experiment is itself the determinant in bringing out the 30 percent of us who in any case rise to uncertainty with a positive outlook.

As for the other two-thirds of us, we will continue, at least initially, to resent uncertainty until we learn how to use it to some good end. But the conclusion that must not be ignored is this: a system that depends upon immediate satisfaction cannot, by definition, induce change, because the maintaining of high levels of overnight success is predicated on your not growing. It's as simple as that and equally plain to see. So long as we market to you a pseudo-challenge that makes you all happy on that final day of class when you fill out your course evaluations, we will make certain that whatever experiences you had at college that molded you into a new person will not be ones that take place in the classroom. After all, we faculty are not likely to be in much of a position anyway to influence your identity.

So, what does all of this have to do with the 1960s, the present marketing of higher education as a consumer commodity, and the current rage for social inactivity? Quite a bit actually, for what it tells us is this: if you are genuinely growing through what you learn in class (and this *is* the big "if" in the current climate), the evaluations you are forced to fill out before you have fully assimilated your experiences will always produce glowing reports in about seven of a class's twenty-four students. In other words, those evaluations are *guaranteed* (at least in an environment of true intellectual growth) to produce a statistic that is miserable enough to ensure the failure of any professor's candidacy for reappointment. What it also tells you, of course, is that the reason our institutions of higher learning today strike us as so unbelievably boring is that they have taken themselves out of the running as potential catalysts for your growth.

After all, a chance is not a chance if not a chance, if you see what I mean. For every baby boomer who took a chance and made it work—who went to Vietnam, or moved to Canada, or dropped out and lived in the woods to some good purpose—there were hundreds who fell off the edge of the planet: who died in Vietnam, whose Canadian experience wounded them permanently, whose hippie lifestyle left them conversing with house pets. This is to say that it is unfair of us in the extreme to expect that colleges and universities should—at least as they are currently designed—be places where we meet the adventuresome souls who are willing to take the kinds of chances that are the precondition for human growth.

Those who live in love of institutions and the safety they provide are the least likely themselves to take the risks upon which personal development depends, and they are, in turn, the least well positioned to understand what we individually may need to sense in order to cope with the uncertain world that awaits us as we grow and learn. It is for this reason, and perhaps for this reason alone, that our colleges have now become the permanent home for the pragmatic bean counter, the upbeat prince, the angry princess, the happy environmentalist, the righteous activist, the consuming student, and those just afraid of living. If all are now caricatures that the modern college cannot live without, some would say we have received our just desserts.

Thus, maintaining some healthy distance from those institutions that inflate their own authority (as a means of limiting the self-confidence that is required to transcend them) provides us with a place to begin our quest for creative revisioning. Culturally driven and individually shared forms of meaning, though often restrictive and coercive in nature, can be employed constructively and, when necessary, transcended when deep domains of meaning are sensuously reorchestrated. Call this ritual, if you will, or call it art. The label applied matters less than the understanding of how creativity flourishes when meaning becomes supra-normal. Elevating misfortune into something having transcendental qualities not only then creates the possibility of bettering the lot of humankind but also opens windows onto a new view of what collective action can become. This creation of beauty out of disadvantage is the stuff of true art. It has happened throughout the course of human history and will happen yet again.

Notes

Chapter 1

1. In *The Age of Immunology* (2003), I describe this model as "thermodynamic," in that hot and cold produce the greatest expression of an energy that, by nature, is ambivalent—in its extreme forms, as much capable of inducing chaos as growth.

2. Indeed, the volume of Wilce (2003) for which a version of this chapter provided a conclusion, was enthusiastically reviewed precisely because its interdisciplinary nature (combining psychology, neurology, and social analysis—that is, PNI!) was not only scientifically provocative but *novel*.

3. For a fuller discussion see Napier 2003.

4. See Granger and Granger 1986.

5. See Gartner and Lipsky 1987.

Chapter 2

1. Understanding the difference between classificatory principles and their social manifestations is central to an appreciation of the views of Durkheim and Mauss (for example, 1903). As Needham has argued, "this distinction, between categorical forms of thought and the process of thinking, was emphasized by Durkheim (1898), and it remains as crucial today as when he formulated it" (1972, 157).

2. The much-misunderstood field of phenomenology actually had its origins in the attempt to transcend the effects of culture upon perception, even though the naiveté of his exercise led Husserl, the "father" of twentieth-century phenomenology, to its opposite—namely, to a poetics of language.

3. Though anthropology's impact on philosophy is arguably quite minimal, even the most Eurocentric of thinkers could not avoid the stranger cases from the ethnographic record.

4. Frazer, after all, was a classicist who achieved fame by cataloging for any curious reader the colonial record.

5. The other recognition only happened in the more recent, so-called reflexive literature that prohibits an author from talking about anything other than his or her impressions or, perhaps, a domain of pedestrian practicality (see, for example, Bourdieu 1972).

6. "One day, when I was moved by the idea, I wanted to measure the progress of

those whom I had taught for many years. So, I said to one of them: 'Essentially, it is the notion of the spirit that we've brought to your thoughts.' 'Not at all,' came the brusque objection. 'We have always known the spirit. What you have brought us is the body.' — ????" For further discussion of this passage, see Napier 1986:17.

7. "A personage is a figure and a [social] role. [The New Caledonian] does not discriminate between the body and the role.

8. Though the literature is extensive, multiple sources can be obtained from my first two books (1986, 1992).

9. Though not by Gregory Bateson (who was extrememly generous) nor my supervisor, Rodney Needham.

10. I had gone to Leuven (the home of Husserl's archives) some years earlier to study phenomenology.

11. Though one could never be certain, for all good magic hides its locus of blame.

12. See Napier 2003, chap. 2, section 3. The controversial literature surrounding the publication in 1994 of Herrnstein and Murray's book *The Bell Curve* is vast; see, for example, Fraser 1995 for a summary and discussion.

13. This argument is made at length in Napier 2003.

14. In *The Age of Immunology*, I claim that the falling out of fashion of the study of cultural categories of thought stemmed in large measure from a misunderstanding of how flexible those categories are and how flexible the meanings are that individuals attached to them in any social setting. In fact, it could be argued that their very flexibility is what allows for their ideological resilience.

15. Similarly critical arguments are made most notably by Jackson (1983a, 1983b, 1989) and Taussig (1992, 1993).

16. This idea has been argued by Ortner (1995). In Ohnuki-Tierney's words, "the notion of the de-essentialized subject reproduces the construct of freely choosing individuals—a decisively Western ideological construct" (2001:247). For an alternative case against essentialism, see Rodseth 1998.

17. Goffman, of course, long ago understood this shared sense of being outside—that is, the way in which we all fall short of an ideal human type that "may be fully entrenched nowhere," yet that casts "some kind of shadow on the encounters encountered everywhere in daily life" (1963:129).

18. For an extended elaboration of this problem, see, for example, Fjellman's extraordinary ethnography of Disney World (1992).

19. Though this cannot be the place to offer multiple examples, I have elsewhere described the nature of such social conditions—for example, for Rome during the Counter-Reformation; for Athens in the sixth century B.C.; for Moscow at the demise of the Soviet Union; or for Hindu Bali in the present day (see Napier 1992). Onuki-Tierney has recently offered compelling comparable cases for Japan and, in the same publication, a critique of Friedman's examples from the Congo (1990); see also Wikan 1996.

20. This uncertainty is the kind that Turner attempted to define through his notion of extended liminality: "What appears to have happened is that with the increasing specialization of society and culture, with progressive complexity in the social division of labor, what was in tribal society principally a set of transitional qualities 'betwixt and between' . . . has become itself an institutionalized state" (1977:107).

21. In a fascinating and much neglected discussion of this comparison, Kenny asks why the widely reported phenomenon of spirit possession is not matched in creative curing through the management of what our ego-oriented world has labeled the "multiple personality."

22. In Japan, for instance, the obvious threat to ethnic integrity posed by the prac-

tice of transplanting organs is reflected in criminal accusations being levied against surgeons who engage in such practices. Lock (2002), for example, describes one of the most famous of recent Noh dramas as revolving around a plot in which a deceased soul whose body was the victim of this practice returns to earth to haunt those responsible for its dissection. See, for instance, Lock 2002; Lock and Honde 1990; Ohnuki-Tierney 1994; and Scheper-Hughes 2000.

Chapter 3

1. Another account of this event may be read in the first chapter of *The Age of Immunology* (Napier 2003).

2. For a more detailed assessment of Latour's argument, see Napier 2003.

Chapter 4

1. Students of Human Ecology is a registered 501(c)3 nonprofit, the purpose of which is to encourage the application of anthropological training for undergraduates to public projects in the areas of health care and the environment.

2. The project, supported by the Vermont State Medical Society and the Vermont Academy of Family Physicians, examined issues of recruitment and retention among a cohort of 242 physicians (Napier 1993).

3. By "social work" what they generally meant was all forms of counseling and any other tasks regularly engaged in that were not biomedically involved.

4. That we are failing in this respect is beyond doubt. Some years ago, as a response to the Clinton-era national concerns about primary care, almost an entire issue of *JAMA* (September 7, 1994) was devoted to medical schools, medical education, and generalist practice (for example, Martini et al.). Yet this issue contained not only no article on the importance of early experiences in decision-making, but also no consideration of any experiences taking place before the first year of medical school. Indeed, we found no suitable existing models for the program we have been operating in Vermont for more than a decade now.

5. That we are motivated by the sensational and the novel is doubtless; yet part of this need to focus on the sensational comes, one might argue, from never really having experienced the tragedies that one finds fascinating. As Lasch points out of writers of the Holocaust, "the siege mentality is much stronger in those who know Auschwitz only at second hand than in those who lived through it" (1984:128). Indeed, the need to visit your personal views of human tragedy on others is often itself a sign that intelligent debate over the causes of such tragedy is no longer possible; "the unseemly eagerness to exploit the victims' suffering for polemical advantage; the refusal to let them rest in peace; the obsessive interest in documenting their ordeal down to the last detail; and the growing insistence that it offers exemplary moral and sociological insights provide an index of the steady decline of this discourse on mass death" (122). In this respect, the absence of interest in subjects that are not readily sensationalized is itself, one could argue, an outcome of not having ever been transformed by human experience.

6. Wytham Hall Sick Bay has become well known for its unusual and highly successful initiative for caring for the homeless. In fact, their success is virtually unparalleled.

7. The project, funded by the Trustees of Wytham Hall, resulted in a long-term study of the hospital and four videos on the subject of homelessness.

8. By comparison it is interesting to note that these percentages are virtually identical to the percentages of individuals who either remain calm in the face of disaster (that is, roughly 2 out of 7) or are stunned or bewildered by such experiences. See J. Leach 1994:24.

9. There is even a company today that uses anthropological methods to garner at-home responses to new consumer products (Osborne 2002). The marketing research firm, Housecalls, employs observational techniques that go back to Craig Gilbert's early reality television show "An American Family." Following Margaret Mead's lead in applying anthropology to everyday America, Gilbert painted a sometime disturbing picture of a single American family by filming their everyday activities for the benefit of PBS viewers (Ruoff 2002). One might say here that this "real life" portrait anticipates not only so-called "reality television," but that other oxymoron of anthropology called "lived experience"; for both presume that a postmodern play life exists that is otherwise not lived.

10. The internships were made possible through grants from the Conanima Foundation and the Justin Brooks Fisher Foundation.

11. A not dissimilar condition of extended transformation is isolated by Luhrman (1989) in her study of the modern-day wicca movement in England.

12. In his inaugural lecture at the London School of Economics, Sennett labeled the appearance of this kind of loss in the contemporary transnational economy as "the incompleteness of capitalist time" (2000:27; see also Sennett 1998).

13. These consequences are, to wit, that one cannot have it both ways—that is, if you say that sick societies produce sickness among its members and that ours is a sick society, you cannot then go about writing books that appeal to the social skills of readers who, by definition, do not have them. Part of the problem with, as we regrettably say, "problematizing" culture is that one rapidly loses the awareness that this attitude is not universally shared.

14. Worth remembering again is Appadurai's previously noted distinction between "hard" and "soft" cultural forms. "Hard cultural forms are those that come with a set of links between value, meaning, and embodied practice. . . . Soft cultural forms, by contrast, are those that permit relatively easy separation of embodied performance from meaning and value" (1996:90).

15. There are compelling biological reasons for this argument. For instance, Walter Cannon noted long ago (1932) the importance of shivering for visceral learning. The absence today of biological stress reduces the body's capacity to adjust to temperature variation. For Cannon then the presence of central heating, warm clothing, and the absence of a stress that "inoculates" and conditions may be responsible for the biological inability to respond effectively to changes in the environment—why, that is, people are always troubled by a so-called "dysfunctional immune system" every time it rains or the weather changes. Biological stress, like social stress, is as much instructive as it may be debilitating.

16. One might note here the shamanic literature in which one's abilities as a healer are correlated with one's having survived a battle with demons in which one is literally torn apart (Kenny 1981). By this view, our best doctors become rural caregivers because they have reconstructed themselves from the smallest pieces to which their education and experiences have symbolically dismembered them.

17. In Bali, for instance, the witch Rangda is well known for inadvertently doing things backwards, causing misfortune and harm even when her intentions might have been otherwise. One historical myth about her (in her form as Calon Arang) even has her thanking the monk who manages to defeat her—for he had, in so doing, released her from her unintended misdeeds.

18. Part of the title for this current section, "Time Out of Time," comes from a book on festivals and transformation edited by Alessandro Falassi (1987).

19. In *Foreign Bodies*, I invent the term "selective dissociation" to describe the willful decision to participate in such transformations (1992:190 ff.).

20. Harsh in that it reminds me not a little bit of Camille Paglia's aggressive challenge that we speak out forcefully against the widespread corruptions of the academy (1992). However, Bourgois (1996) has shown within anthropology itself how such institutional loyalties not only induce a fear of the real world, but also skew our understanding of the lives of those we study.

21. One might sense this change of view by comparing his early interest in the phenomenal power of institutions to his later efforts to adjust creatively to the pathos of living. See, for example, Rabinow 1989 (especially 8 ff.).

Chapter 5

1. The lion's share of medical-school expenses, for instance, comes from grants, endowments, and fees for services (Mechanic, Coleman, and Dobson 1998). Only 3.8 percent of medical school revenues come from student tuition (Krackower et al. 2000) as opposed to, say, seventy years, ago when fees and tuitions covered approximately 34 percent of all operating costs (Lowell et al. 1932). These changing fee structures, combined with the formation of research monopolies (Napier 2002), nearly guarantee some colluding between academics and their so-called not-for-profit employers.

2. Interview with Dr. Beech Conger. For a fuller discussion of this passage and its implications, see the epilogue in Napier 2003.

3. In that year the United States Supreme Court granted rights previously enjoyed by people to corporations, thus allowing knowledge shared by their employees (that is, otherwise common knowledge) to be held as the sole intellectual property of that corporate "person." On the relevance of this event to the controlling of intellectual property by big business, see Napier 2002.

4. Which, of course, as "people," corporations are entitled to enjoy.

5. Any look at the trial records of well-publicized recent prosecutions of corporate CEOs will make the apparent lack of generosity in this statement appear more polite than it ought to be.

6. A look at the various discussions surrounding the work and related projects of Richard Sennett will position one very swiftly in this domain.

7. Some of these amount to as much as 125 percent of actual costs, which means that the research institution gets $1.25 for every $1.00 actually spent on research.

8. Though the critical literature on governmental and nongovernmental aid organizations is vast and rapidly growing, see Blustein 2001 for a readable account of the disasters that can be caused by involution, even within the very institutions created to oversee global financial stability.

9. Though statistics vary, the general rule is that the top 1 percent of the population makes more money each year than the bottom 90 percent. Many of our most powerful corporations pay no taxes, but instead spend those funds on lobbying congressmen, who in turn must spend on average four out of five working hours on reelection fundraising. If small businessmen or individual investors make mistakes, it is hard luck for them, but when our nontax-paying corporations go bottom up, we bail out for the betterment of the nation the ones that fund candidates.

10. "To corporations, the world's rich, and warlords around the world, offshore centers are an indispensable lever for operating global markets. They present a valuable

check on the hunger of the world's governments for tax revenue and their zeal for over-regulation. Offshore centers push international tax and regulatory competition in which all countries must vie against one another to create welcoming environments for the world's corporations and investors. The most lightly taxed and superficially regulated win. 'Tax competition between states is a good thing,' declared the *Wall Street Journal*. 'The power of individuals and companies to vote with their feet is one of the most potent weapons against overweening government. Any attempt to deprive them of places to run must surely be considered an attack on freedom and a threat to prosperity.' . . . The estimates of how much criminal money is entering the world financial system from all sources range between $500 billion and $1 trillion a year. The midpoint of the estimates tops the GDP of Canada. . . . World capitalism does not distribute insight into how many deaths are too many or into how to save a world that profits in its own destruction. Like the tide, it cares not the slightest on which shore we land" (Fishman 2002:39-41).

11. This statement is verbatim from a medical-school admissions committee member who was defending the admission of a candidate with an MCAT score of 17 (a score of 25–30 is the baseline norm of acceptance).

Bibliography

Abram, David. 1984–85. "Sleight of Hand." *Appalachia*, Winter: 10-21.

Adams, Jeff. 1986. *The Conspiracy of the Text: The Place of Narrative in the Development of Thought*. London: Routledge.

Adelberg, Michael. n.d. *The Natural History of Explanation*. Vols. 1–3.

Ader, Robert, David L. Felten, and Nicholas Cohen, eds. 1991. *Psychoneuroimmunology*. San Diego: Academic Press.

Appadurai, Arjun. 1996. *Modernity at Large: Cultural Dimensions of Globalization*. Minneapolis: University of Minnesota Press.

Atwood, Margaret. 1988 (1984). "England: A Field Guide." In *The Armchair Traveler*, ed. John Thorn and David Reuther. New York: Prentice Hall.

Beneke, Tim. 1982. *Men on Rape*. New York: St. Martin's Press.

Berger, John. 1967 (1997). *A Fortunate Man: The Story of a Country Doctor*. New York: Vintage Books.

Berlin, Isaiah. 1968. "Verification." In *The Theory of Meaning*, ed. G. H. R. Parkinson. London: Oxford University Press.

Blustein, Paul. 2001. *The Chastening: Inside the Crisis that Rocked the Global Financial System and Humbled the IMF*. New York: Perseus Books Group.

Bourdieu, Pierre. 1977 (1972). *Outline of a Theory of Practice*. Cambridge: Cambridge University Press.

Bourgois, Philippe. 1996. "Confronting Anthropology, Education, and Inner-City Apartheid." *American Anthropologist* 98, no. 2: 249–57.

Brigham, Deirdre Davis, and Philip O. Toal. 1991. "The Use of Imagery in a Multimodal Psychoneuroimmunology Program for Cancer and Other Chronic Diseases." In *Mental Imagery*, ed. Robert G. Kunzendorf et al. New York: Plenum Press.

Buckler, William E. 1961. *Novels in the Making*. Boston: Houghton Mifflin.

Canetti, Elias. 1960. *Masse und Macht*. (Trans. *Crowds and Power*, 1962.) Hamburg: Claassen Verlag.

Canguilhem, Georges. [1966] 1989. *The Normal and the Pathological*. Trans. Carolyn R. Fawcett and Robert S. Cohen. New York: Zone.

Cannon, Walter B. 1932. *The Wisdom of the Body*. New York: Norton.

———. 1942. " 'Voodoo' Death." *American Anthropologist* 44: 169-81.

Carrithers, Michael, Steven Collins, and Steven Lukes, eds. 1985. *The Category of the Person: Anthropology, Philosophy, History*. Cambridge: Cambridge University Press.

Castaneda, Carlos. 1968. *The Teachings of Don Juan: A Yaqui Way of Knowledge*. Berkeley: University of California Press.

Caudill, W. 1958. *The Psychiatric Hospital as a Small Society*. Cambridge, Mass.: Harvard University Press.

Cone, Richard A., and Emily Martin. 1998. "The Immune System, Global Flows of Foodstuffs, and the New Culture of Health." In *The Visible Woman*, ed. Paula Treichler and Constance Penley. New York: New York University Press. Rpt. in James M. Wilce, Jr., *Social and Cultural Lives of Immune Systems*, London: Routledge, 2003.

Conrad, Joseph. 1937 (1907). "The Secret Agent" (author's preface). In *Conrad's Prefaces*. London: J.M. Dent and Sons.

Csordas, Thomas. 1994. *The Sacred Self: A Cultural Phenomenology of Charismatic Healing*. Berkeley: University of California Press.

Damasio, Antonio R. 1994. *Descartes' Error: Emotion, Reason, and the Brain*. New York: G. P. Putnam.

Danforth, Loring M. 1989. *Firewalking and Religious Healing: The Anastenaria of Greece and the American Firewalking Movement*. Princeton, N.J.: Princeton University Press.

Devlin. Keith. 1997. *Goodbye Descartes: The End of Logic and the Search for a New Cosmology of Mind*. New York: John Wiley and Sons.

DiGiacomo, Susan M. 1987. "Biomedicine as a Cultural System: An Anthropologist in the Kingdom of the Sick." In *Encounters with Biomedicine: Case Studies in Medical Anthropology*, ed. Hans A. Baer. Montreaux: Gordon and Breach.

Donlon, Margaret M., Ori Ashman, and Becca Levy. 2003. "Media and Aging." *Journal of Social Issues*. Forthcoming.

Donovan, Rosie, and John Bain. 2000. *Single-Handed: General Practitioners in Remote and Rural Areas*. Latheronwheel, Scotland: Whittles Publishing.

Dubuffet, Jean. 1988. *Asphyxiating Culture: And Other Writings*. Trans. Carol Volk. New York: Four Walls Eight Windows.

Durkheim, Émile. 1898. "Représentations individuelles et représentations collectives." *Revue de Métaphysique et de Morale* 6: 273–302.

———. 1915. *The Elementary Forms of Religious Life*. Trans. J. W. Swain. London: George Allen and Unwin.

Durkheim, Émile, and Marcel Mauss. 1903. "De quelques formes primitives de classification: contribution à l'étude des représentations collectives." *Année sociologique* 6: 1–72.

Edgerton, Gary. 1994. " 'A Breed Apart': Hollywood, Racial Stereotyping, and the Promise of Revisionism in *The Last of the Mohicans*." *Journal of American Culture: Studies of a Civilization* 17, no. 2: 1-20.

Edgerton, Robert. 1967. *The Cloak of Competence: Stigma in the Lives of the Mentally Retarded*. Berkeley: University of California Press.

Fadiman, Anne. 1997. *The Spirit Catches You and You Fall Down: A Hmong Child, her American Doctors, and the Collision of Two Cultures*. New York: Farrar, Straus and Giroux.

Falassi, Alessandro. 1987. *Time Out of Time: Essays on the Festival*. Albuquerque: University of New Mexico Press.

Festinger, L., H. W. Riecken, and S. Schachter. 1964 (1957). *When Prophecy Fails: A Social and Psychological Study of a Modern Group that Predicted the Destruction of the World*. New York: Harper and Row.

Fish, Stanley. 2002. "Postmodern Warfare: The Ignorance of Our Warrior Intellectuals." *Harper's Magazine* 305, no. 1826: 33-40.

Fishman, Ted C. 2002. "Making a Killing: The Myth of Capital's Good Intentions." *Harper's Magazine* 305, no. 1827: 33-41.

Fjellman, Stephen M. 1992. *Vinyl Leaves: Walt Disney World and America*. Boulder, Colo.: Westview Press.

Fraser, Steven, ed. 1995. *The Bell Curve Wars: Race, Intelligence, and the Future of America.* New York: Basic Books.

Friedman, J. 1990. "Being in the World: Globalization and Localization." *Theory, Culture and Society* 7, nos. 2–3: 311–28.

Foucault, Michel. 1997a."Self Writing." In *Ethics: Subjectivity and Truth*, ed. Paul Rabinow. Trans. Robert Hurley et al. (*Essential Works of Foucault, 1954-84, Volume One*). New York: The New Press.

———. 1997b."Technologies of the Self." In *Ethics: Subjectivity and Truth*, ed. Paul Rabinow. Trans. Robert Hurley et al. (*Essential Works of Foucault, 1954-84, Volume One*). New York: The New Press.

Fussell, Paul, ed. 1987. *The Norton Book of Travel.* New York: W. W. Norton.

Gartner, Alan, and Dorothy Kerzner Lipsky. 1987. "Beyond Special Education: Toward a Quality System for All Students." *Harvard Educational Review* 57 (November): 367-95.

Geertz, Clifford. 1973. "Thick Description: Toward an Interpretive Theory of Culture." In *The Interpretation of Cultures: Selected Essays.* New York: Basic Books.

Gell, Alfred. 1992. *The Anthropology of Time: Cultural Constructions of Temporal Maps and Images.* Oxford: Berg.

Geracioti, Thomas D., et al. 1987. "The Onset of Munchausen's Syndrome." *General Hospital Psychiatry* 9: 405–9.

Gide, André. 1951. *The Counterfeiters, with Journal of "The Counterfeiters."* Trans. Dorothy Bussey and Justin O'Brien. New York: Alfred A. Knopf.

Goffman, Irving. 1963. *Stigma: Notes on the Management of Spoiled Identity.* New York: Simon and Schuster.

Goldman, Irving. 1975. *The Mouth of Heaven: An Introduction to Kwakiutl Religious Thought.* New York: John Wiley.

Good, Byron J. 1994. *Medicine, Rationality, and Experience: An Anthropological Perspective.* Cambridge: Cambridge University Press.

Granger, Lori, and Bill Granger. 1986. *The Magic Feather: The Truth About "Special Education."* New York: Dutton.

Gupta, Akhil, and James Ferguson. 1992. "Beyond 'Culture': Space, Identity and the Politics of Difference." *Cultural Anthropology* 7, no. 1: 6–24.

———, eds. 1997a. *Anthropological Locations: Boundaries and Grounds of a Field of Science.* Berkeley: University of California Press.

———, eds. 1997b. *Culture, Power, Place: Explorations in Critical Anthropology.* Durham, N.C.: Duke University Press.

Guzman, Susanna A. 2001. *Diagnosis and Management of Allergic Rhinitis.* Monograph No. 3. Leawood, Kan.: American Academy of Family Physicians.

Hall, Nicholas R. S., and Maureen P. O'Grady. 1991. "Psychosocial Interventions and Immune Function." In *Psychoneuroimmunology*, ed. Robert Ader, David L. Felten, and Nicholas Cohen. San Diego: Academic Press.

Hallowell, A. Irving. 1955. *Culture and Experience.* Philadelphia: University of Pennsylvania Press.

Halpern, Baruch. 2001. *David's Secret Demons: Messiah, Murderer, Traitor, King.* Grand Rapids, Mich.: William B. Eerdman.

Hammersley, Martyn. 1992. *What's Wrong with Ethnography?: Methodological Explorations.* London: Routledge.

Haraway, Donna. 1991. *Simians, Cyborgs, and Women: The Reinvention of Nature.* New York: Routledge.

Harrington, Anne. 2000. *The Placebo Effect.* Cambridge, Mass.: Harvard University Press.

Harvey, David. 1989. *The Condition of Postmodernity: An Enquiry into the Origins of Social Change*. Oxford: Basil Blackwell.

———. 1991. "Flexibility: Threat or Opportunity?" *Socialist Review* 21, no. 1: 65–77.

Hecht, David, and Maliqalim Simone. 1994. *Invisible Governance: The Art of African Micropolitics*. Brooklyn, N.Y.: Autonomedia.

Hegel, G. W. F. 1977 (1807). *Phenomenology of Spirit*. Oxford: Oxford University Press.

Herrnstein, Richard, and Charles Murray. 1994. *The Bell Curve: Intelligence and Class Structure in American Life*. New York: Free Press.

Homan, Roger. 1991. *The Ethics of Social Research*. London: Longman.

hooks, bell. 1994. *Outlaw Culture: Resisting Representations*. New York: Routledge.

Houseman, Michael. 1998. "Painful Encounters: Ritual Encounters with One's Homelands." *Journal of the Royal Anthropological Institute (N.S.)* 4, no. 3: 447–67.

Houseman, Michael, and Carlo Severi. 1998. *Naven or the Other Self: A Relational Approach to Ritual Action*. Leiden: Brill.

Howe, Leo. 2000. "Risk, Ritual, and Performance." *Journal of the Royal Anthropological Institute (N.S.)* 6: 63–79.

Jackson, Jean. 1990. " 'I am a Fieldnote': Fieldnotes as a Symbol of Professional Identity." In *Fieldnotes: The Making of Anthropology*, ed. Roger Sanjek. Ithaca, N.Y.: Cornell University Press.

Jackson. Michael. 1983a. "Knowledge of the Body." *Man* 18: 327-45.

———. 1983b. "Thinking Through the Body: An Essay on Understanding Metaphor." *Social Analysis* 14: 127-49.

———. 1989. *Paths Towards a Clearing: Radical Empiricism and Ethnographic Inquiry*. Bloomington: Indiana University Press.

Johnson, Mark. 1987. *The Body in the Mind: The Bodily Basis of Meaning, Imagination, and Reason*. Chicago: University of Chicago Press.

Kenny, Michael G. 1981. "Multiple Personality and Spirit Possession." *Psychiatry* 44, November: 337-58.

Kirkaldy, Andy. 2001. "Baseball not Family-friendly." *Addison County Independent*, November 8: 1B.

Kirmayer, Laurence. 1992. "The Body's Insistence on Meaning: Metaphor as Presentation and Representation in Illness Experience." *Medical Anthropology Quarterly* 6, no. 4: 323-46.

Kleinman, Arthur. 1980. *Patients and Healers in the Context of Culture*. Berkeley: University of California Press.

Knauft, Bruce M, ed. 2002. *Critically Modern: Alternatives, Alterities, Anthropologies*. Bloomington: Indiana University Press.

Krakower, J. Y., T. Y. Coble, D. J. Williams, and R.F. Jones. 2000. "Review of US Medical School Finances, 1998–99." *Journal of the American Medical Association* 284, no. 9: 1127–29.

Krupat, Arnold. 1992. *Ethnocriticism: Ethnography, History, Literature*. Berkeley: University of California Press.

Lasch, Christopher. 1984. *The Minimal Self: Psychic Survival in Troubled Times*. New York: W. W. Norton.

———. 1991. *The True and Only Heaven: Progress and Its Critics*. New York: W. W. Norton.

Latour, Bruno. 1987. *Science in Action: How to Follow Scientists and Engineers Through Society*. Cambridge, Mass.: Harvard University Press.

———. 1993. *We Have Never Been Modern*. Trans. Catherine Porter. Cambridge, Mass.: Harvard University Press.

———. 1996. *Petite réflexion sur le culte moderne des dieux faitiches*. Paris: Synthélabo groupe.

Latour, Bruno, and Steve Woolgar. 1979. *Laboratory Life: The Construction of Scientific Facts* (2nd rev. ed. 1986). Princeton, N.J.: Princeton University Press.

Leach, Edmund R. 1961. "Two Essays on the Symbolic Representation of Time." In *Rethinking Anthropology*. London: Athlone Press.

Leach, John. 1994. *Survival Psychology*. New York: New York University Press.

Leenhardt, Maurice. 1937. *Documents Néo-Calédoniens*. Travaux et mémoires de l'Institut d'Ethnologie, 9. Paris: Institut d'Ethnologie.

———. 1937. *Gens de la Grande Terre*. Paris: Gallimard.

———. 1942. "La Personne mélanesienne." In *La Structure de la personne en Mélanésie*. Milan: S.T.O.A.

Lemert, Charles. 1997. *Postmodernism Is Not What You Think*. Oxford: Basil Blackwell.

Lennon, John. 1964. *In His Own Write*. New York: Simon and Schuster.

Lentricchia, Frank. 1990. "In Place of an Afterword—Someone Reading." In *Critical Terms for Literary Study*, ed. Frank Lentricchia and Thomas McLaughlin. Chicago: University of Chicago Press.

Lévy-Bruhl, Lucien. 1949. *Les Carnets de Lucien Lévy-Bruhl*. Paris: Libraire Plon.

Lock, Margaret. 2002. *Twice Dead: The Circulation of Body Parts and Remembrance of Persons*. Berkeley: University of California Press.

Lock, Margaret, and C. Honde. 1990. "Reaching Consensus about Death: Heart Transplants and Cultural Identity in Japan." In *Social Science Perspectives on Medical Ethics*, ed. G. Weisz. Dordrecht: Kluwer Academic.

Lopez, Donald S., Jr. 1998. *Prisoners of Shangri-La: Tibetan Buddhism and the West*. Chicago: University of Chicago Press.

Lovelock, James E. 1990. *The Ages of Gaia: A Biography of Our Living Earth*. New York: Bantam Books.

Lowell, L. A. et al. 1932. *Final Report of the Commission on Medical Education*. New York: Association of American Medical Colleges.

Luhrman, Tanya. 1989. *Persuasions of the Witch's Craft: Ritual Magic and Witchcraft in Present-Day England*. Oxford: Basil Blackwell.

Lutz, Catherine, and Geoffrey M. White. 1986. "The Anthropology of Emotions." *Annual Review of Anthropology* 15: 405-36.

Lyon, Maragret. 1993. "Psychoneuroimmunology: The Problem of the Situatedness of Illness and the Conceptualization of Healing." In *Bio-politics: The Anthropology of the New Genetics and Immunology*. Dordrecht: Kluwer Academic Publishers.

———. 2003. " 'Immune' to Emotion: The Relative Absence of Emotion in PNI and Its Centrality to Everything Else." In James M. Wilce, Jr., ed. *Social and Cultural Lives of Immune Systems*. London: Routledge.

McNicol, Iain. 2002. "Evidence to the Rural Working Group of the NHS Confederation's New Contract Negotiations." Unpublished working paper.

Mander, Jerry. 1978. *Four Arguments for the Elimination of Television*. New York: William Morrow and Company.

Mann, Samuel J. 1996. "Severe Paroxysmal Hypertension: An Autonomic Syndrome and Its Relationship to Repressed Emotions." *Psychosomatics* 37: 444–50.

———. 1999a. *Healing Hypertension: A Revolutionary New Approach*. New York: Wiley.

———. 1999b. "Severe Paroxysmal Hypertension (Pseudopheochromocytoma): Understanding Its Cause and Treatment." *Archives of Internal Medicine* 159: 670–74.

Marchand, Roland. 1998. *Creating the Corporate Soul: The Rise of Public Relations and Corporate Imagery in American Big Business*. Berkeley: University of California Press.

Martin, Emily. 1994. *Flexible Bodies: Tracking Immunity in American Culture—From the Days of Polio to the Age of AIDS*. Boston: Beacon Press.

Martini, Carlos J. M., et al. 1994. "Medical School and Student Characteristics That

Influence Choosing a Generalist Career." *Journal of the American Medical Association* 274 no. 9: 661–68.

Massey, Irving. 1969. *The Gaping Pig: Literature and Metamorphosis*. Berkeley: University of California Press.

Maturana, Humberto R. 1980. *Autopoiesis and Cognition: The Realization of the Living*. Dordrecht: D. Reidel.

Mauss, Marcel. 1935. "Les Techniques du corps." *Journal de Psychologie normal et pathologique* 32: 271-93.

———. 1938. "Une Catégorie de l'esprit humain: la notion de personne, celle de 'moi' " (Huxley Memorial Lecture, 1938). *J.R.A.I.* 68: 263–81.

Mechanic, R., R. Coleman, and A. Dobson. 1998. "Teaching Hospital Costs: Implications for Academic Missions in a Competitive Market." *Journal of the American Medical Association* 280, no. 11: 1015–19.

Meštrović, Stjepan G. 1992. *Durkheim and Postmodern Culture*. New York: Aldine de Gruyter.

Mironko, Charles. Forthcoming. *Justice Reform and Gacaca Courts in Rwanda*. Ph.D. dissertation, Yale University.

Moerman, Daniel E. 2000. "Cultural Variations in the Placebo Effect: Ulcers, Anxiety and Blood Pressure." *Medical Anthropology Quarterly* 14, no. 1: 51–72.

———. 2002. *Meaning, Medicine and the "Placebo Effect."* London: Routledge.

Mullan, Bob. 1995. *Mad to Be Normal: Conversations with R. D. Laing*. London: Free Association Books.

Napier, A. David. 1986. *Masks, Transformation, and Paradox*. Berkeley: University of California Press.

———. 1992. *Foreign Bodies: Performance, Art, and Symbolic Anthropology*. Berkeley: University of California Press.

———. 1993. "Listening to Vermont's Physicians." *Vermont State Medical Society Reporter*, September: 7-10.

———. 2002. "Our Own Way: On Anthropology and Intellectual Property." In *Exotic No More: Anthropology on the Front Lines*, ed. Jeremy MacClancy. Chicago: University of Chicago Press.

———. 2003. *The Age of Immunology: Conceiving a Future in an Alienating World*. Chicago: University of Chicago Press.

Narby, Jeremy, and Francis Huxley, eds. 2001. *Shamans Through Time: 500 Years on the Path of Knowledge*. New York: Penguin Putnam.

Needham, Rodney. 1972. *Belief, Language, and Experience*. Oxford: Basil Blackwell.

Nichols, B. 1981. *Ideology and the Image: Social Representation in the Cinema and Other Media*. Bloomington: Indiana University Press.

Ohnuki-Tierney, Emiko. 1994. "Brain Death and Organ Transplantation: Cultural Bases of Medical Technology." *Current Anthropology* 35, no. 3: 233–54.

———. "Historicization of the Culture Concept." *History and Anthropology* 12, no. 3: 213–54.

Ortner, Sherry B. 1984. "Theory in Anthropology since the Sixties." *Comparative Studies in Society and History* 26 no. 1: 126–66. Reprinted in Nicholas B. Dirks, Geoff Eley, and Sherry B. Ortner, eds., *Culture/Power/History: A Reader in Contemporary Social Theory* (Princeton, N.J.: Princeton University Press, 1994).

———. 1989. *High Religion: A Cultural and Political History of Sherpa Buddhism*. Princeton, N.J.: Princeton University Press.

———. 1995. "Resistance and the Problem of Ethnographic Refusal." *Comparative Studies in Society and History* 37, no. 1: 173–93.

Osborne, Lawrence. 2002. "Consuming Rituals of the Suburban Tribe." *New York Times*, January 13: 28–31.

Paglia, Camille. 1992. "The Nursery-school Campus: The Corrupting of the Humanities in the US." *Times Literary Supplement*, May 22: 19.

Payer, Lynn. 1988. *Medicine and Culture: Varieties of Treatment in the United States, England, West Germany, and France*. New York: Henry Holt and Company.

Peele, Stanton. 1985. *The Meaning of Addiction: Compulsive Experience and Its Interpretation*. Lexington, Mass.: D. C. Heath.

Pennebaker, J. W., and A. Graybeal. 2001. "Patterns of Natural Language Use: Disclosure, Personality, and Social Integration." *Current Directions in Psychological Science* 10, no. 3: 90–93.

Perry, John, ed. 1975. *Personal Identity*. Berkeley: University of California Press.

Phillips, Adam. 1994. *On Flirtation*. Cambridge, Mass.: Harvard University Press.

Pollock, Donald. 1996. "Training Tales: U.S. Medical Autobiography." *Cultural Anthropology* 11, no. 3: 339–61.

Rabinow, Paul. [1989] 1995. *French Modern: Norms and Forms of the Social Environment*. Chicago: University of Chicago Press.

Rabinowitz, H. K., J. J. Diamond, F. W. Markham, and N. P. Paynter. 2001. "Critical Factors for Designing Programs to Increase the Supply and Retention of Rural Primary Care Physicians." *Journal of the American Medical Association* 286, no. 9: 1041–48.

Rhodes, Richard. 2002. *Masters of Death: The SS-Einsatzgruppen and the Invention of the Holocaust*. New York: Alfred A. Knopf.

Ricoeur, Paul. 1992. *Oneself as Another*. Trans. Kathleen Blamey. Chicago: University of Chicago Press: 1992.

Rider, Mark S., and Cathy Weldin. 1990. "Imagery, Improvisation, and Immunity." *Arts in Psychotherapy* 17, no. 3: 211–16.

Rider, Mark S., et al. 1990. "Effect on Immune System Imagery on Secretory IgA." *Biofeedback and Self-regulation* 15, no. 4: 317–33.

Rodseth, Lars. 1998. "Distributive Models of Culture: A Sapirian Alternative to Essentialism." *American Anthropologist* 100, no. 1: 55–65.

Ruoff, Jeffrey. 2002. *An American Family: A Televised Life*. Minneapolis: University of Minnesota Press.

Satel, Sally. 2000. *PC. M.D.* New York: Perseus Books Group.

Scheper-Hughes, Nancy. 2000. "The Global Traffic in Human Organs (with comments)." *Current Anthropology* 41, no. 2: 191-224.

Schieffelin, E. L. 1996. "On Failure and Performance." In *The Performance of Healing*, ed. C. Laderman and M. Roseman. London: Routledge.

Schor, J. B. 1998. *The Overspent American: Why We Want What We Don't Need*. New York: Harper Collins.

Seligman, Adam B. 2000. *Modernity's Wager: Authority, the Self, and Transcendence*. Princeton, N.J.: Princeton University Press.

Sennett, Richard. 1998. *The Corrosion of Character: The Personal Consequences of Work in New Capitalism*. New York: Norton.

———. 2000. "Cities without Care or Connection." *New Statesman* 129, no. 4489: 25–27.

Shapiro, Andrew. 1992. *We're Number One: Where America Stands—and Falls—in the New World Order*. New York: Random House.

Shattuck, Roger. 1996. *Forbidden Knowledge: From Prometheus to Pornography*. New York: St. Martin's Press.

Shostak, Marjorie. 1983. *Nisa: The Life and Words of a !Kung Woman*. New York: Random House.

Spencer, Jonathan. 1989. "Anthropology as a Kind of Writing." *Man*, March: 145–64.

Stiglitz, Joseph E. 2002. *Globalization and its Discontents*. New York: W. W. Norton.

Stoller, Paul. 1989a. *Fusion of the Worlds: An Ethnography of Possession Among the Songhay of Niger*. Chicago: University of Chicago Press.

———. 1989b. *The Taste of Ethnographic Things: The Senses in Anthropology*. Philadelphia: University of Pennsylvania Press.

———. 1997. *Sensuous Scholarship*. Philadelphia: University of Pennsylvania Press.

———. Forthcoming. *Stranger in the Village of the Sick: A Memoir of Cancer, Sorcery and Healing*. Boston: Beacon Press.

Stone, Deborah. 1993. "Clinical Authority and the Construction of Citizenship." In *Public Policy for Democracy*, ed. Helen Ingram and Steven Smith. Washington, D.C.: Brookings Institution.

Taussig, Michael. 1992. *The Nervous System*. London: Routledge.

———. 1993. *Mimesis and Alterity: A Particular History of the Senses*. London: Routledge.

ten Have, H. 1987. "Medicine and the Cartesian Image of Man." *Theoretical Medicine* 8 no. 2: 235–46.

Turner, Victor. 1964. "Betwixt and Between: The Liminal Period in *Rites of Passage*." In *The Proceedings of the American Ethnological Society, 1964*. Seattle: University of Washington Press.

———. 1977 (1969). *The Ritual Process: Structure and Anti-Structure*. Ithaca, N.Y.: Cornell University Press.

Valenti, F. Miguel. 2000. *More Than a Movie: Ethics in Entertainment*. Boulder, Colo.: Westview Press.

van Gennep, Arnold. 1960 (1909). *The Rites of Passage*. Trans. Monika Vizedom and Gabrielle Caffee. Chicago: University of Chicago Press.

Varela, Francisco J. 1991. *The Embodied Mind: Cognitive Science and Human Experience*. Cambridge, Mass.: M.I.T. Press.

Walsh, Roger. 1984. *Staying Alive: The Psychology of Human Survival*. Boulder, Colo.: Shambhala Publications.

Weck, Wolfgang. 1976 (1937). *Heilkunde und Volkstum auf Bali*. Jakarta: P.T. Bap Bali and P.T. Intermasa.

Wikan, Unni. 1990. *Managing Turbulent Hearts: A Balinese Formula for Living*. Chicago: University of Chicago Press.

———. 1996. "The Nun's Story: Reflections on an Age-Old, Postmodern Dilemma." *American Anthropologist*, 98, no. 2: 279–89.

Wilce, James M., Jr., ed. 2003. *Social and Cultural Lives of Immune Systems*. London: Routledge.

Williams, Melissa S. 1998. *Voice, Trust, and Memory: Marginalized Groups and the Failings of Liberal Representation*. Princeton, N.J.: Princeton University Press.

Zachariae, Robert, et al. 1994. "Changes in Cellular Immune Function After Immune Specific Guided Imagery and Relaxation in High and Low Hypnotizable Healthy Subjects." *Psychotherapy and Psychosomatics* 61, nos. 1–2: 74–92.

Index

Abram, David, 50
addictive stimulus, social setting and, 7
Ader, Robert, 1, 7
Aka-Evy, Jean Luc, 94
alienation: love of, 37; time, 66; writing about, 66–67
ambivalence: fear and, 69; risk and, 67; stress and, 69; transformation and, 8
amodernity, 37
anaphylaxis, 40–41
anthropological paradox, 39
anthropology: animism in, 16–17; appropriating experience by, 43; cultural constructs in, 14–15; education and, 47; ethnography and, 55; imitation in, 49; medicine and, 42–52; Munchausens's-by-proxy and, 50; narrative of, 74, 78–79; networks of power and, 45–46; nonordinary and, 39; ordinary knowledge and, 39–40; Other in, 24; participant-observation in, 50; reflexive, 55; ritual in, 9; rules in, 53; shared perceptions in, 14; social, 14; subjects of, 47, 50; suffering and, 43; transformation and authority for, 55; writing, 55
anxieties: behaviors of, 65; life-enhancing, 34; self-censorship caused, 76
Appadurai, Arjun, ix, 31
appropriation, xi–xii; experience and, 44, 48; traits eroded by, 48
Aristotle, 22, 74
Ashman, Ori, 87
attachment, place of, x
Atwood, Margaret, 46, 47

Bateson, Gregory, 16
behavior: pathological, 65; values versus, 30; war and, 103
beliefs, influence of, 10
bell curve, 21
Berger, John, 78–79
bias, experiential considerations and, 21
Boas, Franz, 16
body: disintegration and refabrication, 36; French society and, 23; *la terrain* as, 23–25
The Body in the Mind (Johnson), 11
Byron, Lord, 54

Canetti, Elias, 44
Cannon, Walter B., 5, 10
canons, 48
career: decision-making, 59; early experience and, 58–59, 111n4
Carnegie, Andrew, 88
Cartesian, 6–7; diseases, 10; ideals, 15
Castaneda, Carlos, 51
catharsis. *See* transformation
Caudill, William, 49
change, x–xi, xiii–xiv; absence of, xiii; behavioral inversions of, 65; creativity by, 106–7; denying the possibility for, 63–64; dissociation and, 68; expectations of, 36; external agent and, 63; fear of, 67; illness and, 7; institutional complacency and, xi; liminality signal of, 82; narratives of, 69; nature of, 6, 28; personal, 97; personhood and, 6; psychological, 82; resistance to, xi, 86; risk essential to, 69, 82; social factors and, 6; stress and, 1–3, 7–8, 82; structure of, 28; temporal experience of, 82, 97;